Magic and Mystery in Ancient Egypt

Magic and Mystery
in
Ancient Egypt

Christian Jacq

Translated by
Janet M. Davis

SOUVENIR PRESS

Contents

List of illustrations   9

1 **Eternal Magic**   11
   The Intuitive Heart   17
   A State Magic   18
   The Magician King   20
   Famous Magicians   22
   Magic Texts   24
   Sacred Archives and Libraries of Magic   28

2 **The Magician, Man of Knowledge**   34
   How does one become a Magician?   36
   The Light of the Magician   42
   The Magician as Astrologer   44
   Closely Guarded Secrets and Ritual Requirements   45
   The Divine Tribunal, the Guardians of the Doors,
      the Ferryman   48
   Going Forth by Day   50

3 **The Powers of the Magician**   53
   Magic in the Temples and in the Towns   55
   Conquering Death   56
   The Name, Key to Magic Power   60

4 **The Tools of Magic**   65
   Amulets   65
   Gold and Precious Stones   68

Knots and Numbers   69
The Substitute Body   70
Letters to the Dead   71
The Lamp   73

5   **Mastery of the Elements**   75
Water and the Barque   75
Air   79
Fire   80

6   **The Magician in the Presence of the Gods**   84
Thoth, Master of Magic   84
From Horus to Bes   87
The Goddesses of Magic   91
Dwarfs and Giants   95

7   **The Magician's Battles**   96
Tales and Legends   96
The Battle Against the Enemy   103
Threats   113
The Dangers of the Night   115

8   **Magic and Medicine**   117
A Doctor Magician   117
Blood and Magic   125
Headaches   128
Stomach aches   130
The Eye and the Ear   132
A Heavenly Food   136
Magical Plants   139

9   **Magical Love**   141
Spells   141
Magic and Childbirth   143
The Child   146

10   The Animal World   150
     The Falcon, the Cat and Company   150
     The Scarab   153

Appendix: Egyptian Magic and Christian Magic   165

Epilogue   169

     List of Abbreviations   171
     Bibliography   173
     Notes   177

List of Illustrations

Pharaoh and Isis (Piankoff, *The shrines of
Tut-Ankh-Amon*) 21
Metternich Stela (Fletcher Fund, 1950, 50.85
Metropolitan Museum of Art) 27
Papyrus Salt 825 (British Museum) 30
Rays of light penetrate a mummified being (Piankoff,
The shrines of Tut-Ankh-Amon) 37
Netherworld figures (Piankoff, *The shrines of
Tut-Ankh-Amon*) 43
Isis and Nephthys (Guilmand, *Tombs of Rameses IX*) 46
A Middle Kingdom Coffin 51
House of Life (Derchain, *Le Papyrus Salt 825*) 58
Magic symbols (Piankoff, *The shrines of
Tut-Ankh-Amon*) 66
Magical rituals (Piankoff, *The shrines of
Tut-Ankh-Amon*) 73
The king pouring water (Guilmand, *Tombs of Rameses IX*) 77
Baboons (Guilmand, *Tombs of Rameses IX*) 81
Solar barque (Piankoff, *The shrines of Tut-Ankh-Amon*) 83
Seth and Horus (Guilmand, *Tombs of Rameses IX*) 90
Nekhbet and Wadjet (Piankoff, *The shrines of
Tut-Ankh-Amon*) 94
Regions of the other world (Guilmand, *Tombs of
Rameses IX*) 98
Six fearsome genies (Piankoff, *The shrines of
Tut-Ankh-Amon*) 108
Nedj-Her (Piankoff, *The shrines of Tut-Ankh-Amon*) 123

That which is above is as that which is below
(Piankoff, *The shrines of Tut-Ankh-Amon*)   126
People walking upside down (Guilmand, *Tombs of
Rameses IX*)   131
Celestial Cow (Piankoff, *The shrines of
Tut-Ankh-Amon*)   151
Phases of mutation of creative energy (Piankoff, *The
shrines of Tut-Ankh-Amon*)   160
The energy of growth and resurrection (Guilmand,
Tombs of Rameses IX)   163

1 Eternal Magic

Even today an Egyptologist must be open to adventure and be willing to follow his instincts. Of course we have to spend long hours in libraries, bent over papyri or studying the texts from temples and stelae. In these caverns of buried treasure, thanks to the work of our predecessors, we can weave together the threads which can be spun into new knowledge. But however indispensable these long years of study may be, nothing can replace contact with Egypt itself.

Desiccated theory is all that one can expect from a sceptical attitude towards Egyptian religion, and inevitable if an Egyptologist lacks sympathy with its civilisation. Even in the sciences, intellectual brilliance alone can achieve nothing without sudden leaps of awareness. The greatest scientists are those who have some insight into the mysteries of the universe and attempt to express this knowledge or understanding which matures over the years.

If this is true of the pure sciences like physics, as Eisenberg, Einstein and so many others have shown, it is even more vital in Egyptology if students are to avoid the trap of examining their subject with icy reason and historical 'detachment' alone.

One Christmas evening, at Luxor, I received a gift beyond price: an invitation to dine with a family of snake charmers. The grandfather, a francophile, was fluent in my language. He gave me the place of honour by his side for the meal, with his wife, his four sons and three daughters. Outside the night was balmy. The setting sun blazed out in dozens of colours, fading gradually to a flush of red which died on the walls of the temple of Luxor, the masterpiece of Amenophis III and his brilliant architect, Amenhotep, son of Hapu.

There was nothing regal about my host's house. Poorly furnished though attempting to be stylish, it was nevertheless a shrine to friendship. Grilled pigeons, rice, pancakes ... a feast had been assembled in honour of the traveller.

That Christmas, a Christian festival, our conversation during the course of a long meal, which lasted almost until dawn, turned on one subject only, magic. My host and his sons practised an extraordinary profession as catchers of snakes and scorpions. To the journalists who came from time to time to interview them about their bizarre calling they gave the impression of being simple folk, cautious, the heirs to an old family tradition; they were sellers of poison, a lucrative business. These statements did not satisfy me. In the course of my studies I had, like all Egyptologists, come across magic. Many 'scholars' have tried to weed it out of Egyptian religion as an irrelevance, incompatible with the grandeur of the metaphysical ideas found in the great texts. But magic is stubborn. It is present everywhere in Egypt, in the turn of a story thought of as 'literature', as much as in the interiors of tombs and on the walls of temples. In the time of the pharaohs, those who dealt with poisonous creatures were magicians who had been initiated and were privy to a knowledge, employing specific spells whose use demanded that they be very well qualified.

I reminded my host of these things. He smiled. 'One must acknowledge,' he admitted, 'that it is not within the capacity of everyone to be the brother of a snake ... indeed, perhaps, some magic is useful.' Observing the rules of oriental courtesy, we had embarked on a genuine exchange of ideas.

Convinced that my host must still know and practise the rules of ancient Egyptian magic, I compared his experience with my own knowledge of Egyptology. Thus was born this book on the magic world of pharaonic civilisation. Between the ancient texts and the living experience there was no hiatus; which is why it is possible today to tackle a subject which previously was taboo.*

* In the notes, the reader will find references to Egyptian texts which, unfortunately, are accessible only to specialists. These are the basic material of the written evidence which, when completed by oral information, often turns out to be the key.

Hermopolis, the ancient city sacred to Thoth, patron of Egyptian magicians, like Hermes to the Greeks, is today just a pile of ruins. Here and there, however, traces of its former greatness remain. Of these the most impressive is the tomb of Petosiris, high priest of Thoth and initiate of the mysteries. This tomb is not sacred to death but to eternal life. Its wonderful texts were written to help man fulfil himself, to find deep within himself the truth without which there can be no happiness on this earth. On one of the walls of the tomb you can read these words: 'He who abides in the path of God passes his whole life in joy, blessed with more wealth than all his peers. He grows old in his city, he is a man respected in his province, all his limbs are young like those of a child. His children are before him, of great number and counted among the leaders of their town; his sons succeed him from generation to generation . . . At the last he comes joyfully to the burial place, embalmed in beauty through the work of Anubis.'[1]

To attain the wisdom evoked by the high priest Petosiris good intentions were not enough. A special knowledge, which the Egyptians called 'magic', was an essential prerequisite. This key concept, which today is confused with black magic, sorcery, psychic powers and other more or less alarming phenomena, had a precise meaning in the time of the pharaohs.

It is not possible to separate magic and religion. Can we imagine a ritual without the influence of magic? Don't the religions of the book (Christianity, Judaism, Islam), however much they may sometimes deny it, exert a magic over the human soul, enabling it to reach out to the realities that our senses cannot grasp?

The Egyptian scribes wrote thousands of pages which have been gathered into collections known to Egyptologists as 'magico-religious texts'. A quick and therefore superficial reading of these writings suggests that the Egyptians had certain specific aims: to have a long life on earth, not to lack food in the Netherworld, not to die from snake bite or the sting of a scorpion, to have good health on earth, to rejoice in their physical skills, to enter and leave by the eastern doors of the sky (that is to say, to

have a spirit sufficiently developed to be able to 'circulate' in
the cosmos), to know the souls of the inhabitants of the West
(that is, to have access to the mysteries of the Ancients). Material
wishes and spiritual aspirations, as we can see, are mingled. This
is one of the essential characteristics of Egyptian thought. There
is a heaven, there is an earth. One affects the other. Our earthly
life, in all its most ordinary aspects, is shot through with a spiritual
force which the Egyptians called *heka*, 'magic'. This term, whose
etymology is uncertain, probably signifies 'to control the
powers'—effectively the summit of the magician's art. A man
who wishes to be a magician must be aware of the powers which
rule all life and try them out in practice. No man can become a
magician by himself; as we shall see, the apprentice-magician is
moulded in the specialist schools of the temples, under the guid-
ance of watchful masters who do not allow him to do as he
pleases or to follow his fancy.

For the wise men there was one essential truth—that magic,
understood as a creative force, was created before the world as
we know it. It is the daughter of the sun god whose every ray
of light is a manifestation of magic, for it brings life. To the
ancient Egyptian, everything has life. To think of something as
inanimate proves that our eyes are not truly open to reality. Man,
like any other speck of life, is the outcome of an interplay of
forces. Will he submit to them passively or seek to identify
them? The quality of his fate will depend on his answer to these
questions. The forces of magic only appear hostile to us because
of our lack of knowledge. The modern scientist is quick to criti-
cise primitive people who go into ecstasy or tremble before natural phenomena which they believe to be supernatural. But this
same scientist, despite all his learning, remains a slave of shadowy
regions which may tax the steadiest and most logical mind.
Today's men, like those of yesterday, are faced with the
unknown—the beginning and end of their existence. The magicians of ancient Egypt have much to teach us in this sphere.

The supernatural force which maintains life is not beyond the
grasp of human intelligence. It dwells in the heart of man's being,
in his inner temple. In discovering and using it, the magician is

aware that his action has repercussions in this world and the other, as if there were no real barrier between the two. By knowing the god of magic, he unveils the power of powers and enters into the happy company of the gods. At death, too, he who passes to the other side of the mirror must conserve his magic power to attain the ultimate reality.

This magic can perhaps be defined as the essential energy that flows through both the divine and human spheres. There are no 'living' and no 'dead', only beings who are more or less able to capture that energy which is contained in the secret names of the gods. Learning hieroglyphs, 'the words of the gods', is the way to acquire knowledge of those names and the energy they hold. In Egypt there is nothing intellectual, in its pejorative sense meaning divorced from reality. That is why each magically and ritually animated object—for example, the royal crowns—holds a vital secret. Spirit and matter are woven from the same substance. The important thing in the practice of magic is to identify the thread that links everything and unites all creatures in a chain of cosmic union.

The above explanation is enough to show that the magic of ancient Egypt cannot be regarded as so much jiggery-pokery. In fact we are looking at a sacred science that requires specialists trained for many years to grasp the most secret forces of the universe. According to one magnificent text, *The teachings of Merikare*, 'the Creator gave man magic to repel the thunderbolt of what is to come'. In other words, we are all tied to a predetermined fate. Most of the time, events, whether happy or unhappy, take us by surprise. We are not the masters of our own destiny. The Egyptians do not deny this predestination, but consider that it is possible to escape it by the use of magic. By the practice of that art we can modify our fate and fight against the negative trends in the human lot, whether individual or collective, so avoiding the pitfalls that we see ahead.

In Egypt, magic was regarded as an exact science. Although some amateurs, such as the village witch-doctors, used simple magic spells, the great magic of Egypt was only revealed to an elite of scribes whom we can compare to today's atomic scientists. This magic, in fact, is intended to maintain the world order. It owes nothing to improvisation or some conjuring trick, but depends on a precise sequence of actions which are controlled by the magician.

Human existence hangs in a precarious balance. Many perils threaten it: demons, negative forces, zombies, many manifestations of the 'evil eye'—in other words, a negative energy which, by its power alone, destroys everything that exists. The first duty of a magician is to dam up this negativity and to preserve life. But equally he must take care that the moments of 'passage' unfold correctly. Birth, marriage, death, the ending of the old year and the beginning of the new, are all examples of very delicate situations where the intervention of magic is indispensable.

The magicians freely confess that their secrets go back to remote antiquity. This is not just a convention, but a real need to refer back to the primordial models, the Creation Myths. In some ways, the magician is in direct contact with the architect of the universe. Each magic act is, by definition, an act of creation with its roots deep in the beginning of the world. The magician 'remakes as it was in the beginning', he places 'the first time' in the present, he restores the world 'in that time'. Magical time is primeval time. In the study of magic we reach for the spark from which all creation sprang.

The god of magic, 'Heka', is a creation of the light. It seems inappropriate to speak of 'black' or 'white' magic. In reality there is only one magic, that of the sun, the bearer of light, which brings enlightenment to the magician. All else is conjuring, sorcery, or the quest for power.

In the world of the gods, the god of magic has a precise function: to ward off those things which must be kept at a distance, to prevent evil and disharmony from disturbing the order of things. The magician, when he is truly imbued with divine force, also fulfils this function. He is Horus. The magic of his mother Isis is in his limbs.[2] He is Re of the mysterious names, he is the one who was in the ocean of energy at the dawn of time.[3] He identifies himself with the greatest gods of the pantheon by feeling magic in his own body like a living force. It circulates in his feet, in his hands, in his head, in his entire body. It is clearly stated that the magic force emits light and, on occasions, gives off a characteristic odour.

'Behold, I am one with that magic power, wheresoever it may be, in the house of any man where it is' says the magician in Spell 24 of *The Book of the Dead.* 'It is faster than the hare, swifter than light.' The magician fills his belly with magic power; by its virtue he slakes his thirst.[4] This 'magic in the belly' rises eventually to the spirit, as a fluid circulates in the secret veins of the body. Thus the magician, the son of Re, lord of light and the sun, and of Thoth, incarnated as the moon, reveals the breadth of his perception. His wisdom is passed on in a document which comes from the dwelling of the sun god, having first been sealed in the palace of Thoth.

Without magic, survival is impossible. To those who present themselves at the gates of death the proper spells give enough courage and knowledge to enable them to pass through the barrier without being overwhelmed. The magician travels the sky. Before Orion, he states that he has eaten the powers of life and has been filled with the spirits of the ancient gods whose secret names he knows. Orion hears the traveller from the beyond. He sees that he has indeed assumed all the powers and has forgotten none of them.[5] That is why the reborn, in the form of a star, will shine high in the heavens. Such is the destiny of a magician: to become a light in the cosmos, to light the path of other men.

The Intuitive Heart

Magic is a matter of perception and the centre of keenest perception is the heart. Not the fleshly organ, but the insubstantial centre of being. This heart, according to the Egyptians, is the witness to a man's life. It is impossible to lie to it or to deceive it. This heart-conscience imagines, thinks, commands the nerves, muscles and limbs. It enables the senses to function as they should. Everything comes from the heart and returns to it, it sends forth and it receives. Feelings and impressions are brought back to it so that it can amalgamate them and learn from the information it gleans from the outside world.

According to the mythology of the city of Memphis, the god Ptah conceived the world in his heart before spitting it forth with his tongue. In each sentient being there awakens a heart which is the heir of the divine heart. It holds the divine power, and answers for the righteousness of the magician as he faces his judges, here and in the world beyond. The quality of his magic is directly linked to the quality of his heart. It is for the magician to develop his intuitive faculties which will allow him to discover the mysterious casket of knowledge, which foreshadows the Grail. His heart will tell him how to open it, so that he may find there the essence of magic.

One particular amulet, the heart scarab, plays a decisive role during the passage from life on earth to eternal life. The scarab is the symbol of metamorphoses and changes. In placing it on the heart of the mummy, the magician confers upon it the power to cross the darkest regions where a being is in danger of being overcome by fierce attacks. On his happy arrival on the shores of paradise the heart of the just man will be restored to him. This gift is prepared on earth during the life of an individual. The purpose of magic is to make a heart of heavenly origin beat within him, to awaken his perception of the invisible.

A State Magic

The practice of magic was regarded as fundamental by the state of Egypt. The books of magic are not the scribblings of fantasists but rather the work of official institutions such as the House of Life, and form part of the royal archives. One of the first objectives of magic, in fact, is to protect the pharaoh from all negative influences. In the words of the Egyptologist Jean Yoyotte, 'it is a high state magic, coherent, rational, admirably striking and serene, from which springs the Egyptian view of the world.'[6]

It would be a great mistake to believe that magic in the time of the pharaohs was a matter for the individual. In that form it shows itself at its most decadent and least rich in meaning. Above all the Egyptians used temple rituals, which were performed throughout the land. Each act of worship is magic. For example, only the pharaoh has the ability to control the rites necessary to maintain the presence of the gods on earth. The image of the king, carved upon the walls of each temple, comes to life magically to enter the soul of the priest who actually performs the ceremony.

The greatest centre of magic in Egypt was probably the holy city of Heliopolis, the city of the sun (north of Cairo), where the most ancient theology developed. Here were preserved numerous papyri, 'magic' in the widest sense of the word, including medical, botanical, zoological and mathematical texts. Most Greek philosophers and savants travelled to Heliopolis to study some of that knowledge which had been gathered over the centuries. It was there, notably, that Plato heard the legend of Atlantis, which has caused so much ink to flow and whose true meaning, still misunderstood as far as we know, can only be deduced from the Egyptian texts.

The first principle of magic is that offerings must be made to the gods. This rite ensures that life will continue to renew itself. 'Give Maat (universal harmony) to the Master of Maat (the Creator)'—by following this ritual formula, life may go on.

The ancient Egyptians feared nothing more than chaos, that negative state which is the opposite of Maat, the order of things. Good intentions are not enough to avert the disorder which is the final doom of every civilisation. Magic is a weapon of extraordinary strength. Because of it the solar barques maintain their heavenly orbit, the dead receive the nourishment that is their due, the state functions and the festivals are celebrated. Without the magical intervention of the state, the inundation of the Nile would fail, the fields would not be irrigated, the hunters would not kill game, the fishermen would not catch fish, workmen would not finish their tasks and the temples would not fulfil their role.

Such a viewpoint is surprising to us. Today so many phenomena appear 'natural' to us that we do not perceive their hidden significance. For example, to the Egyptian the hunt was a very special experience during which he entered into a world of unknown forces, beyond human control. Danger was ever-present in the form of a desert creature or a furious crocodile. The hunter's role was to confront the forces of evil, and also to use magic spells to overcome them.

The Magician King

The pharaoh of Egypt has neither father nor mother. He lives life and does not suffer death. He is the great magician *par excellence*, for he is the incarnation of the life force. In the Old Kingdom, only the pharaoh has the right to intercede with the gods on behalf of mankind and, as master of both the natural and the supernatural, he is therefore all-powerful. He acquired this status by eating the magic forces in the course of an extraordinary banquet amid a cosmic upheaval which marked his arrival in the heavenly realms.[7] The stars are darkened. The light is quenched. Heaven and earth tremble. The cause of these events is a terrifying figure—the pharaoh himself. It is he who feeds on his fathers and mothers. He is the master of wisdom whose name is unknown even to his own mother. His glory is in the sky, his power is in the horizon like that of Atum, the Creator who made him. The king has become more powerful than him. Bull of the sky, he assimilates the being of each divinity. He eats men and gods. Khonsu, a fearful genie, kills those of whom the king has need and extracts the contents of their bodies for him. Another genie, Shesemw, cooks them for him on the hearth stones. The king eats their magic, consumes their spirits. The fat are eaten at the morning meal, the medium sized for dinner, the little ones for supper. The pharaoh takes possession of the hearts of the gods, eats the Red crown, and swallows the Green. The whole cosmos acknowledges his supremacy. He feeds on the kidneys of the wise and on their magic. The length of his life is eternity.

This text has been termed a 'cannibal hymn', in the belief that it refers to very ancient rituals in which the Egyptians would have consumed human flesh. However, it actually describes the acquisition of magic power by the straightforward ingestion of divine vitality seen as food.

Filled with magic, the pharaoh is protected. Any evil being

Pharaoh, protected by Isis, approaches Osiris. The goddess wears the hieroglyphic sign for a throne on her head, thus defining her symbolic nature. She is the throne-goddess from whom the kings are born. From her right hand she pours a fluid onto the pharaoh's nape, one of the vital centres of his person. With her left hand she supports the king's right arm, a magical action which is necessary because pharaoh is grasping the two sceptres which give him the power to exercise his sovereignty over the world of men. The pharaoh is clothed in his robes of office: the double crown (made up of the white crown of Upper Egypt and the red crown of Lower Egypt), the nemes wig and ceremonial loin-cloth. In front of Osiris is a small altar upon which stand an incense burner and some flowers. The king is offering the god of resurrection the essence of all things.

who bites him will only succeed in poisoning itself. Each part of the royal body has become divine. The pharaoh's belly for example, is Nut, the goddess of the sky. Now, the magic power is precisely located in this 'heavenly belly'.

Standing before the gods, the pharaoh wields his authority. He orders them to construct a staircase so that he may climb to the sky. If they do not obey him, they will have neither food nor offerings. But the king takes one precaution. It is not he himself, as an individual, who speaks, but the divine power: 'It is not I who say this to you, the gods, it is Magic who addresses you.'[8]

When the pharaoh completes his ascent, magic is at his feet.[9] 'The sky trembles,' he declares, 'the earth shivers before me, for I am a magician, I possess magic.'[10] It is also he who installs the gods on their thrones, thus proving that the cosmos acknowledges his omnipotence.

In Egypt of the Old Kingdom, everything about the royal person had a magical quality. As the pharaoh is the only priest, it is his task to 'charge' the state rituals with magic. The royal name is contained in a 'cartouche' whose Egyptian name *snw* means 'that which encircles' (that is, the container of the Universe over which the pharaoh reigns). By the use of puns, which are fundamental to the understanding of hieroglyphic language, this term also implies the idea of 'conjuration'. The royal name is also magically protected by the cartouche. Emblems, insignia, royal garments, all are charged with magic, especially the crown. It is regarded as a living being, a goddess, at once a fierce lion and a serpent who attacks the king's enemies. Hymns are sung to it. Only the pharaoh can wear it and use its secret powers.

Famous Magicians

According to Manetho, the priest of Sebennytos, who in the Greek period devoted a celebrated work to the history of the kings of Egypt, the pharaoh Athothis (1st Dynasty) was a doctor who wrote books of anatomy. He also practised magic, setting a precedent for his successors. In view of this, it seems likely that all pharaohs were magicians as part of their office.

In the Old Kingdom, Imhotep was the most celebrated of magicians. His fame was such that, several centuries later, the Greeks identified him with their own god of medicine, Asclepios. By the time of the New Kingdom, worship of the 'god' Imhotep had become a cult among the scribes; before starting to write they would make a libation in memory of their patron. Imhotep, indeed, is a key figure to our understanding of the importance of magic as an art in ancient Egypt. This man was no peasant sorcerer but the first Minister of the mighty pharaoh, Djoser, and the inventor of stone architecture, whose masterpiece was the step-pyramid at Saqqara. In other words, a statesman of the first rank for whom skill in magic was judged indispensable for the proper conduct of his duties. Some 'recipes' attributed to Imhotep have been passed down to posterity, such as this one:[11] 'Take an olive wood table with four feet. Place it in the centre of a pure place; cover it completely with a cloth. Place four bricks beneath the table, one on top of the other, and in front of the table, a silver censer. Put charcoal made from olive wood in the censer and goose fat minced with myrrh and shaped into small dumplings, and recite a spell. Speak to no one throughout the night. You will see the god in the form of a priest dressed in a linen robe.' Thus the magician invokes him who sits in the shadows, surrounded by the great gods, seeking and receiving the rays of the sun.

Hardedef, one of the sons of Cheops, was known for his extensive knowledge and wise sayings. He discovered several ancient books of magic, whose formulas are included in the written rituals. Khaemwaset, the fourth son of the famous pharaoh Rameses II, was the high priest of Re at Memphis. He built and restored many monuments and had a passion for archaeology and the study of ancient documents. He was regarded as a very wise man and inspired two stories of magic to which we shall return.

Horus, son of Panesh, was a magician of the Late Period. He had to contend with an Ethiopian sorcerer who threatened the security of the state. This Horus had lived fifteen centuries previously and had been reincarnated to save his country.

It is to the magician Es-Atum, a priest who lived at the time of Nectanebo II (359–341 BC) that we owe the survival of the famous *Stela of Metternich*. Es-Atum had discovered that some-one had removed an inscription from a temple of the sacred city of Heliopolis. So that this valuable evidence should not be lost, he had the text recopied onto a stela which has come down to us.

This brief survey is simply intended to illustrate the continuity of the status of the magician throughout Egyptian history. There are of course scores of others one could name—for example, Harnuphis who was the last really famous Egyptian magician. He was present on the field of the battle of Mordavia in AD 172, with the army of Marcus Aurelius. There was a shortage of water and, lacking supplies, the Romans were in danger of dying of thirst. The Egyptian caused rain to fall, astonishing the barbarians and saving the soldiers of Marcus Aurelius. Thus the ancient knowledge of the land of Egypt demonstrated that it had lost none of its effectiveness.

Magic Texts

The magic texts, which make up a large part of Egyptian 'litera-ture', were written on a variety of materials: papyrus (from the time of the Middle Kingdom), ostraca (fragments of pottery), stelae, statues, many small objects. Modern scholars, accustomed to categorising everything, have fallen into the habit of classifying Egyptian texts as 'literary', 'religious', 'magical', and so on. These formal distinctions do not correspond to the reality. *The Tale of the Shipwrecked Sailor*, known as 'literature', is a wonder-ful story of magic. The *Coffin Texts*, labelled 'funerary', con-stantly call on magic. In as much as any text written in hieroglyphs thereby acquires a power of its own, one could say that all Egyptian writing is magical although obviously this is truer of some texts than of others.

Certain texts, however, stand out for their importance or origin-ality. Amongst these the *Book of Two Ways*, written on a Middle Kingdom sarcophagus, gives the dead man knowledge of the ways of the Underworld. Two paths, one of earth, one of water, are separated by a river of fire. These are the symbolic ways to enter a country peopled by dreadful genies. A kind of Grail is there, which the just find after undergoing many trials to which only knowledge of magic can provide the keys.

The *Books of Hours* are collections of spells which the magician recites throughout the hours of day and night to placate the gods. The *Bremner-Rhind Papyrus*, which describes the struggle of the powers of the sun against the monstrous dragon Apophis, a genie of darkness, also contains an esoteric treatise on the nature of god. It tells us that the Master of the Universe created all living creatures at a time when the earth did not yet exist. The plan of creation was conceived in his heart. From being One, the architect of the worlds became Three. He set in motion changes and transmutations and made his abode on the primeval mound, the first land to emerge from the waters. As for men (*remetj*), they were born from the tears (*remetj*) of the god when he wept over the world.

The *Stela of Metternich* is the most celebrated of the many magical stelae. It dates from the fourth century BC and contains a remarkable text which tells of the magical healing of the infant Horus when he was stung by a poisonous creature in the marshes of the Delta, where he lived in secret with his mother Isis. On the front of the stela, in the upper part, is Horus, standing on crocodiles and grasping the venomous creatures. The young god is protected by Thoth the magician and by Hathor, goddess of harmony. Above, a symbolic 'cartoon strip' shows seven panels featuring gods and genies performing rites to invoke the powers of magic. At the top of the stela, eight baboons serenade the birth of light. The *Stela of Metternich* also shows the role of Isis, the great enchantress. When she found her son Horus in agony, she appealed to the inhabitants of the marshes but none of them knew the appropriate remedy. No one could speak the words that could heal. Would Atum, the Creator, let his life be extinguished? Isis took Horus from the coffin in which he lay and screamed loud and long to the heavens. Her threat is terrifying: if her son is not healed, light will no longer shine. The heavenly powers, thus forced to respond, intervene on behalf of the young god. 'Awake,

Horus,' they say. The poison loses its power to harm and becomes ineffective. Horus is healed. Order is restored to the world. The divine barque sails anew through the expanse of heaven.

Another surprising inscription is on the 'healing statue' of a person called Djed-Her, the guardian of the doors of the temple of Athribis. Discovered in 1918 and now in the Cairo Museum, it tells us about religious practices in the fourth century AD. Standing on a plinth 65cm (26in) high, this black granite monument is in the form of a crouching figure, his arms crossed and his back against a pillar. His body is covered with inscriptions except for the face, hands and feet. The surface of the plinth is hollowed out so that two basins, joined by a channel, catch the water which is imbued with magic by being poured over the statue. By drinking this water, the sick are healed.

On each healing statue, it is important that the name of the dead person be mentioned. The deceased asks that those who wish to use his statue for magic purposes should read the ritual texts for his sake. He also appears as a saviour who performs miracles. 'O, ye priests,' says a text on the statue, 'ye scribes, ye wise men, may all of you who look upon this Saviour recite his writings, know his magic spells. Keep his writings, protect his magic spells. Tell of the funerary offerings which the king gives, a thousand good and pure things for the *ka* (the vital power) of this Saviour who has made his name Horus-the-Saviour.'

On the base of a statue of black granite (32.3cm (13in) long, 12cm (4in) high) which was acquired by the Leyden Museum in 1950, is a similar inscription covered in magic texts; it dates approximately from the Ptolemaic period. It reveals that Isis, having left the secret dwelling where Seth had taken her, drew on all her magical knowledge to cure a child who unfortunately had been stung by one of the seven scorpions which preceded her in her travels.

Among 'magic' statues, one that stands out is that of the pharaoh Rameses III which was found in the eastern desert.[12] Its purpose was to protect travellers from poisonous animals, especially snakes. Those who ventured into the waters of the Suez isthmus also benefited from the favours of the divine Rameses III

On the Stela of Metternich, which is an important text worth studying for its
own sake, there is what can only be described as a magical 'cartoon strip'.
At the top of the stela are eight baboons worshipping the rising sun, whilst
Thoth directs the ritual. It tells the story of the magical creation of light and
the struggle against the forces of darkness, symbolically depicted in the
lower bands of the stela. The central figure is that of Horus, represented as
a naked child, standing on crocodiles and holding poisonous and dangerous
animals in his hands. The young god, fears no danger and masters the
power of evil, because he is protected by many divinities, notably by Bes,
whose enormous smiling head is a pledge of safety.

whose effigy, placed in a small oratory, blessed the passer-by. Magic spells which, in assuring the safety of the infant Horus also guaranteed that of the traveller, were carved on the statue (or more precisely on the group of sculptures, for the king was accompanied by a goddess).

A guild of magicians, the *Saou*—that is, 'the protectors'— was deputed to safeguard those who followed the tracks across the desert. Rameses III had a particularly close rapport with the world of magic. During the sombre criminal affair known as 'the Harem Conspiracy' (a plot hatched by his ministers) the blackest magic was used in an attempt to do away with the head of State. One of the conspirators had managed to uncover a highly secret magic text in the royal archives. The plotters fashioned waxen images representing the pharaoh's guard and succeeded in paralysing them. They no doubt hoped to go further and harm the pharaoh himself, but they were identified and captured. The use of magic as a weapon in crime was deemed a capital offence, the sentence to be executed by suicide.

Many museums hold papyri of varying degrees of interest. The *Bremner-Rhind Papyrus* has already been discussed, and one could draw up a long list of documents (many of them unpublished, untranslated, or still inaccessible for reasons which are often obscure). One of these, the *Demotic Papyrus of London and Leyden*, enjoys a reputation which it scarcely deserves. This document, of very late date, actually mixes the practice of divination, spells of simple sorcery and fragments of ancient mythology. It reflects a side of magic which shows very little coherence and concentrates on charms, many aimed at winning the favour of a sweetheart. In any case, this papyrus was written not only for the use of the Egyptians but also for the Greeks and Christians.

Sacred Archives and Libraries of Magic

In Egypt, sacred writings are called *Baou Ra*, 'the powers of the god of Light'. Books, explains a papyrus,[13] are the power of the god of Light through which Osiris lives. It is by means of these sacred archives that the great divine powers, Re, the god of Light, and Osiris, Lord of the Shadowlands, communicate. Men are not the authors of the magic books, but Thoth, the master of the sacred words, Sha, the god of wisdom, and Geb, the lord of the earth. In their writings, they pass on to mankind the information it is capable of using.

The magician must therefore have a perfect knowledge of the divine world. At the pinnacle of his art, he is regarded as the Master of the Ennead, the primordial group of nine gods which was at the start of all creation. As wearer of the great crown, the magician becomes the interpreter of sacred texts. Egyptians love the written word. It records knowledge. 'Love books as you love your mother' is the command given to those who seek wisdom. The magician is not content to read: he swallows the texts, puts pieces of papyrus in a bowl, drinks the magic Word, ingests the words that hold meaning. This extraordinary rite was passed down to the guilds of the cathedral masons.

Next to the mummy a papyrus was placed, to repel hostile forces and allow the deceased to enter the unknown regions of the nether-world in complete safety. These magic writings were placed, sometimes near the head, sometimes near the feet, and sometimes between the legs of the mummified corpse. In this way the deceased had useful spells and itineraries at his disposal and signposts which would guide him well on his posthumous journey.

Each temple housed a library of magic containing works needed for ritual practices and the confidential teachings of prac-titioners. At Edfu, for example, were works on fighting demons, driving off crocodiles, appeasing Sekhmet, hunting lions and pro-tecting the king in his palace. The magician ordered his life by cosmic laws: 'the twentieth day of the first month of the inun-dation is the day for receiving and sending letters. Life begins and ends on that day. It is the day for compiling the book 'The End of the Work'—a secret book, which binds spells, which hinders plots, which threatens the whole universe. It contains both life and death.'[14]

Magical writing enjoys a life of its own for it is written in hieroglyphs, signs that carry power. The *Pyramid Texts*, which consist of numerous magic spells, provide a very important

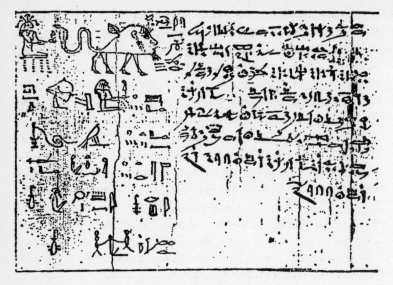

*An example of a magic text: a page of the Papyrus Salt 825 in which the
ritual of the House of Life is revealed. On the left is hieroglyphic writing
with various symbols, on the right, 'hieratic' writing, a cursive form of the
same.*

example of this. These texts, written on the inner walls of the
pyramids of the Old Kingdom (5th and 6th Dynasties), appear
in the form of columns of hieroglyphs. Each hieroglyph is
regarded as a living being, so much so that dangerous or unclean
animals (for example, lions and snakes) are cut in two or mutilated
so that they will not harm the dead and reborn king. Even in the
composition of these texts can be seen the familiar practices, like
that of compiling long lists of vanquished foes or the parts of
the dead man's body that are identified with those of gods. Incomprehensible words are also used, arranged for effect into patterns
of sounds; they are a mixture of Egyptian, Babylonian, Cretan
and other foreign languages to make a sort of 'abracadabra'.
These weird aberrations of sacred magic should not make us
forget the power of the word. When they are intoned these magic
spells take on a real potency of their own. The hieroglyphic
language is very largely founded upon a sacred 'alphabet' which
represents the basic phonograms (or sounds), consonants and

semi-consonants. The vowels are not written. They are changing, perishable elements, dependent upon time and place. To compensate, the 'framework of consonants' is the constant element of the language. This idea of the magical value of language lasted a long time; an amulet of the Coptic era contained twenty-four magic names, each beginning with one of the letters of the Greek alphabet.[15]

'I am the Great Word,' declares the pharaoh,[16] meaning that he can give life to all things. There is a secret word in the shadows.[17] Every spirit who knows it will escape destruction and dwell among the living. The traveller from beyond, discovering it, dons the magician's robe that gives him the right to godlike status. Whoever possesses the formula will be able to wield his own magic.[18]

When the gods speak, they rend the void and open the way to the forces of life. That is why the magician repeats the words of the gods, such as those of Horus, which banish death, quench the poison's fire, restore life and save mankind from an evil destiny. The words and spells used by the magician are not a matter of chance; they are inspired by sacred legends, by deeds from divine ages which are repeated in the world of men. The most powerful spells are the oldest—those, in fact, that stem from the dawn of life—and the greatest of all, *peret kherou*, means 'that which is spoken'. The Word alone can give life to matter.

The general title of a magic spell is 'Spell for . . .' becoming, being, having power over. It must be read, recited, learnt, understood, inscribed, and used as a true spiritual and material tool. To repeat a magic text four times makes it totally effective, but equally crucial are the tone, rhythm and the way it is chanted.

For the magician, how he utters that spell which, combined with gestures, makes up an act of magic, is the key. By giving it life he enchants the sky, the earth, the powers of night, the mountains, the waters, and understands the language of the birds and reptiles. Everything hangs on it. The proper recitation of the spells will enable him to follow the path of Osiris and become a part of that brotherhood of the gods of Upper and Lower Egypt, the most closed society of initiates imaginable.

Even the gods themselves are forced to obey the magician's words of power: 'Oh, all you gods and goddesses, turn your face towards me! I am your master, the son of your master! Come with me and bear me company ... I am your father! I am a companion of Osiris, I have travelled through every part of the sky, I have burrowed through the earth, I have crossed the world between, following in the steps of the Enlightened ones, for my store of magic spells is without number.'[19]

The magician believes that his words and his appearance give him power. Having crossed the horizon and travelled throughout the heavens, he has received the teaching of the blessed ones.

The one for whom the spells are recited benefits from important privileges; he drinks the water of the river, emerges by day like the god Horus, lives as a god and is worshipped by the living as a sun.[20] He who recites the proper spells can go everywhere. Whatever form he assumes, he will be steadfast.[21] He will cast his seed upon the earth. and have heirs who will continue his work. Neither his power nor his shade will be the prey of demons. And that, add the authors of the books of magic, is 'the truth a million times over.'

There is even a spell to give protection from death whatever the cause—illness, wild animals, drowning, the bone of fish or bird, hunger, thirst, or aggression, human or divine.[22] Indeed, a constant war must be waged against the unseen foe and its innumerable guises. So the magician keeps reciting the complicated spells that will save him from the dreadful fate of asphyxiation.[23] Lack of air seems to have been one of the obsessions of the Egyptians for whom breathing was the most obvious sign of life.

Magic also protects the just man from being eaten by serpents. His best form of protection is to assume the shape of a serpent which could itself devour its own kind.[24] We shall come back to these themes which are typical of Egyptian magic.

State magic, private magic: the two terms are not contradictory, but their aims are very different. The first attains a cosmic dimension, the other, often in initiation, is constantly at risk of falling into errors that lead to powers of the most terrible kind. Aren't we the same, with the scientific disciplines of which we are so proud?

Egyptian magic is a vision of the world which illuminates both the light and dark sides of the human mind. Long before the coming of psychoanalysis it was a fruitful means of learning about the ultimate reality that lies within us. Although not without danger, it was also used for manipulating a psychic energy which, tentatively and with some surprise, the most rational scientists are now beginning to rediscover.

Ancient Egypt has much to teach us in the domain of magic, as in many other fields. Let us listen, then, to the magicians as they speak of their certainties and their fears, celebrate their successes and discuss how they might fail. Their experiences are ours, too.

2 The Magician, Man of Knowledge

An Egyptian family man who is also a magician observes a daily ritual within the bosom of his family. When there is a family reunion for a festival or special occasion, the father truly becomes the symbol of a supernatural power. No one may approach him at all or speak to him at any time. In the west we have lost this sense of the sacred in our simplest actions. But, in the words of Hermes Trismegistus, 'That which is below is like that which is above.' Although this opinion may shock some people, I believe that a feast like the one held that Christmas Eve in Luxor is a sacred ceremony.

'The magician,' said my host, 'is a man who knows things.' His sons nodded their heads. I did not hide my surprise. 'Knows things'—that seemingly trite expression occurs frequently in hieroglyphic texts. In a magical sense it means the gods on earth. 'Knowledge,' continued the magician of Luxor, 'is the key-word of the art of magic.'

Those who do not know the magic spells will be unable to move around freely in this world or the next. Ignorance nails man to the earth and reduces him to slavery. The magician is 'informed' by Sha, keeper of the knowledge of causes, and Hu, the Creating Word. They take him by the hand and lead him to a mysterious chest. They open it in his presence. Thus the magician sees what is inside it—the very secret of magic.[1]

Intuition and the Word—are these not even today, as in days gone by, the two essential 'tools' of the seeker? From the snake-charmer of the Luxor countryside to the most 'advanced' atomic physicists, is not the process the same—to perceive by intuition and to express by the Word?

The magician is not a necromancer or a follower of the occult. To the Egyptians he is a scholar and a priest. He reads and writes hieroglyphs, and knows that the ancient Spell 572 of the *Coffin Texts* was written to give magic power to him who travels in the kingdom of the dead. He must appeal to the group known as the Followers of Horus, the wisest of the wise, who know the secrets of creation. They protect the magician wherever he may be, so long as he is quick to learn and does not allow himself to forget the books and spells of power. He is a priest because he knows, and as an emblem of his official role he carries a papyrus scroll, symbol of the abstract and of esoteric knowledge.

We, who associate magic with fortune-tellers at garden fêtes or with the most bizarre practices, find all this baffling. But in the civilisation of Ancient Egypt the magician is a public figure who is part of the 'normal' world. What is 'abnormal' is to live without magic, in other words, with our ears and eyes blocked. The magician, a man fitted for the highest office, occupies an important place in the pharaoh's court.

In the villages the local magicians, guardians of the secret arts that are in constant use for the good of all, are leaders of their community, to whom the people always turn for help and advice. They possess the knowledge without which none may feel safe.

As priests, the magicians receive a priestly initiation. Those at the top of the hierarchy are subject to a way of life which Porphyrius described in this way:[2] 'By contemplation, they attain respect, spiritual salvation and piety; by reflection, knowledge; and by the use of both, the practice of secret and time-honoured ways.' We must remember that the chief of the magicians is pharaoh himself, he who wears the crowns that bear the most concentrated and effective magic.

It is the magician's access to knowledge that entitles him to claim: 'I am the master of life in whom life is eternally renewed, and my name is He who Lives the Rites.'[3] In his role as *Khery-heb*, a title meaning 'he who is responsible for the book of rituals', he reads the sacred texts aloud, bringing them magically alive and filling them with power.

In the secret rooms of the House of Life the magician was initiated into the art of reading and understanding the sacred texts which were used in public and private ceremonies. There was a House of Life near each temple so that no part of the country was without specialists who were responsible for this most important skill of government—the practice of the rites.

Several figures stand out among the official body of magicians, notably that of the high priest of Heliopolis, whose Egyptian title *wer maaw* means 'great seer' or 'He who sees the Great (god)' His ritual vestment is a tawny skin spangled with stars which is not unlike the celestial cloak worn by the kings of France at their coronation. The high priest of Heliopolis, 'the supreme master of the secrets of the sky', is the guardian of the most ancient solar traditions and of a magic of the light which watches over the daily rebirth of the life force. Without magic, in fact, the sun would not rise each morning.

The priests of the lion-goddess Sekhmet are not only magicians, but specialists in medicine and surgery. As both medical practitioners and sorcerers their healing skills range from ordinary insect stings to the most serious wounds. Their humblest followers are the village healers who can administer first aid. The work force of builders at Deir el Medina, to whom we owe most of the temples and tombs of the New Kingdom, engaged a charmer of snakes and scorpions to guard against possible accidents.

Magic cannot be separated from those activities which we call 'artistic'. Thus, the sistrum players, dancers and musicians who are on the staff of the temple, do not spend their lives indulging in sensual pleasure but bathe the souls of the gods in streams of harmony, so that they will care for the balance and serenity of mankind.

Nothing is pointless in the ancient Egyptian world of magic. It is all a play of subtle interrelationships which only those initiated into magic can perceive.

How does one become a Magician?

This vital question cannot be answered by giving a 'List of Instructions'. The practice of magic is not licensed by a diploma

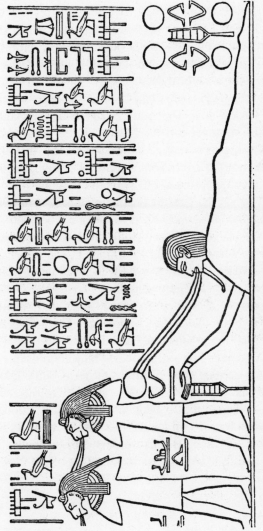

Rays of light penetrate the mouth of a mummified being who is stretched on the ground. The risen man may then speak the Word, shown by the outstretched arm, the symbol of action, over the threshold.

nor by passing an exam. Modern learning has been reduced almost entirely to a series of rules and does not, alas, take any account of practical experience. This was not the case in a civilisation such as Egypt's.

Certainly, there is a way to become a magician, but it cannot be approached rationally. The texts do not hide it entirely but they appeal to our intuition and our inner intelligence rather than to our deductive or analytical faculties.

Spell 261 of the *Coffin Texts* has the title 'To become a magician'. This is what it says. The graduate addresses the magicians who are in the presence of the Master of the Universe. He demands their respect because he knows them, since they guided his steps. Is he not the one whom the Sole Lord created before life on earth was apportioned into twos, the day and the night, good and evil, when the Creator opened his one eye in his solitude? The magician presents himself as the one who controls the Word. He is the son of the Great Mother, she who gave birth to the creator who, nevertheless, has no mother. The father of the gods is the magician himself. It is he who gives them life.

A strange text, indeed. There is nothing here about basic technique; it is actually a treatise on metaphysics and spirituality which throws light on the process of creation. The only practical directions are that the graduate remained silent during the ceremony of enthronement, bowed, and seated himself in the presence of his masters, described as the 'Bulls of the Sky'. They acknowledged his rank as 'possessor of power' and heir of the Creator.

The graduate has come to take his seat on his throne and receive the insignia of his office. All that came into being before the gods belongs to him. He also orders them to come down from the sky and follow in his train as a mark of deference.*

---

* We know of an initiation recounted as an act of birth, thus (*The Leyden Magical Papyrus, 55*): 'I am the face of the Ram. Youth is my name. I was born beneath the revered Persea-tree at Abydos. I am the incarnation of the great noble who is in Abydos (i.e. Osiris), I am the guardian of the great body (of Osiris) who is in Wupek (the sacred place at Abydos).' In other words, the graduate has participated in the reconstitution of the scattered body of Osiris, thus proving his abilities before identifying himself with the reincarnated god.

Qualification as a magician is gained following an interview with the masters of the art, who judge the candidate on his knowledge of the secret love much more than on his practical skills, which will be developed later. In the same way that the dead, having reached the condition of a being of light (the *akh*), rediscovers life at its source, so the graduate succeeds, while still alive, in communing with the light of the very beginning of things, which contains magic in its absolute purity.

The first revelation granted by the masters is that every human problem which faces the magician has a counterpart in the divine world. The same event has occurred on the cosmic ladder before it is felt on earth. That is why the magician must know the genealogy of the gods, theology, and the various myths of the creation of the world. In them he will find a solution to every problem.

By identifying himself with the four cardinal points, the graduate becomes the cosmos—an excellent method of knowing the laws, capturing the invisible powers and directing them at will—partially at least. During the ritual of investiture, the magician is stripped of his 'ego', his too-personal vision of the world, so as to allow the cosmos to penetrate within him. Perhaps drugs were used to plunge him into a trance during which the Brothers magically charged him with energy in preparation for his future tasks.

The invisible powers show themselves in the shape of good or evil genies. The graduate is confronted by them. Once again, he identifies himself with them, which is the best method of getting to know them and gaining the maximum magical power. He can then fight the hell-bent genies and drive them from the body of a sick man. When the demons attack a human, a city, or a field which has been protected by a magician of quality, they come up against no mean adversary.

What can the magician do but invoke the aid of a higher power? The common formula of the magic texts reveals this to us: 'It is not I who says this, it is not I who repeats it, but the god who speaks and just as certainly the god who repeats it.'[4]

Thus it is not the magician who speaks but the divine power who speaks through him. In the struggle of 'good' against 'evil', there is no confrontation between a human and 'something' more than or superhuman, but a duel between some of the supernatural forces, real beings, incarnated in the spirit and body of a magician. The patient himself, whether he is a sick man to be cured or a medium to be 'manipulated', is identified with a divinity who cannot be destroyed. What better assurance could there be of escaping a too cruel fate?

Apuleius, author of *The Golden Ass*, a remarkable initiatory novel in which the mysteries of Isis and Osiris are evoked, was a renowned magician. In his work, he relates the bewitchment of Lucius, who was transformed into an ass. He had to make a long journey before recovering his human form. Only initiation into the mysteries would deliver him from the prison of his animality. Apuleius was troubled by the judicial authorities of his time. In a public trial he was accused of sorcery, and had to use all his powers of oratory to escape conviction. Now Apuleius had some knowledge of Egyptian magic. 'It is,' he wrote, 'an art that is pleasing to the immortal gods, one of the first things to be taught to princes.'[5] In fact, in the course of his ritual 'education' pharaoh is identified with the divinities in a magical way.

A ritual declaration is made to the one who becomes a master of magic:[6] 'You mingle with the gods of the sky and there is no discernible difference between you and them. Your body is that of Atum (the Creator) for eternity.' How better could one affirm that the magician attains the highest sphere of the spirit? There he is impregnated with power, so that he becomes fit to speak with the forces of the cosmos. He is moreover a 'cosmonaut', to use an anachronism, exploring the unknown world after a long physical and psychical pre-paration.

The result of this experience has been piously recorded in texts from various collections: 'There is no part of me that is separate from a god,' explains the magician, 'Thoth is the protection of all my limbs. Every day I am Re ... men, gods, the blessed, the dead, no noble, subject or priest could lay hands on me.'*

To make it clearer, each part of the magician's body is formally identified with that of a divinity. For example, his head is that of Atum, his right eye is that of the same Atum when he disperses the twilight, his left eye is that of Horus who pushes back the day of the new moon when there is a risk of a bad lunar month, his nostrils are those of Thoth and of Nut (the goddess of the sky), his mouth is that of the Ennead of Atum, the group of nine divinities who rule the cosmos, his lips are those of Isis and Nephthys, his fingers are serpents of lapis-lazuli, his vertebrae are the backbones of Geb, the god of the Earth, his belly is that of Nut, his feet are the soles of Shu, the god of the luminous air, when he crosses the sea. To sum up: 'There is no part of him which can be separate from the god who sets his seal on his outline, even when the amulets of Heliopolis are laid on him.'[8]

This obscure statement deserves comment. To the Egyptian, to set a seal is to inscribe the divine on the real. Royal seals are known from the first dynasty. Later on, the most famous of them took the form of a scarab, symbol of becoming. In other words, when the king makes a decision and seals it, he is aware of the outcome, the consequences of his act. A similar awareness is absolutely essential in magic if one is not to lose one's way. The placing of the 'amulets of Heliopolis' refers to a key moment in the initiation of the magician. Recognised as fit for office, his body is reclothed in the insignia of power by the master magician who presides over the ceremony. The amulets are therefore called 'of Heliopolis' because that ancient city of the sun was the centre of magic. They are also arranged on the mummy to make it incorruptible. This is one of the deep meanings of mummification: to identify mortal remains with an immortal body so that the soul, armed with this support, can enter the Netherworld in a state of knowledge.

Every dead man who has been mummified according to the

---

* This text has many variants. For example: 'There is in me no limb which is separate from the god and Thoth is the protection of my body; my flesh is in the fulness of life, every day . . . 'He who endures for thousands of years' is my name. In every sense I walk the heavens and the earth, the fear that I inspire rules over the entrails of the gods' (Goyon, *Rituels*, 257).[7]

rites becomes a magician capable of rebirth. The Egyptian does not rely on faith alone to avoid the problem of ceasing to be. To him, knowledge seems a better approach.

The Light of the Magician

When the magician looks up at the sky he sees Re, the god of light. When he looks down at the earth he sees Geb, prince of the divinities and the earth-god. These two divinities help him to exorcise evil.[9] Re's cooperation is particularly valuable: thanks to the sacred light, he sees all and disperses the darkness.

Re has the power to change death to life. He repeats this magical act each morning, in the lake of flames, in a bitter struggle against his enemies who try to prevent the light giving life anew. The magician also wages this war against the powers of darkness,[10] first during the ceremony of initiation, then in his daily activities. He needs the divine light to become the one who lights Egypt, the two lands, red and white, the one who drives away the darkness; to become the Bull of the mountains of the East and the Lion of the mountains of the West, the one who every day crosses the expanse of the heavens. When he opens his eye, the light dawns. When he closes it night spreads over the earth. The gods do not know his true name.[11]

Identified with the light on its long journey, the magician clears a path for the sun so that it may travel in peace.[12] So he collaborates with the sun in its daily work and in the regeneration of humanity.

In ancient Egypt, the most developed state of being, which crowns the initiate's path, is *akh*, the luminous, shining personality with supernatural powers. The body belongs to the earth, the *akh* to the sky. It is this being of light which Re reveals to the magician who is able to look at the sun and discover the divine in his contemplation of the star of day. Much later, those who had been initiated were called the 'Enlightened'; today, the term has become a pejorative one. A better name would be 'son of the light', an Egyptian expression which defines pharaoh by naming his true father and giving his role a supernatural dimension.

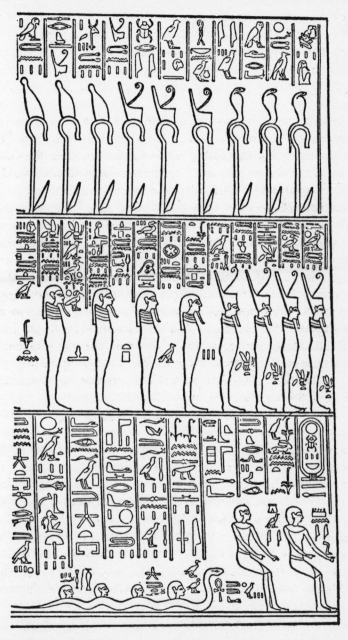

Figures from the other world: beings of human appearance, crowned with royal crowns, a serpent whose body is studded with human heads, objects formed from crowns, sceptres and knives. There are so many items of knowledge and signs to identify on the traveller's path.

The Magician as Astrologer

Egyptian astrology is one of the most difficult and most neglected fields of research.* 'There is perhaps no land,' writes Diodorus Siculus,[13] 'where the order and movement of the stars are observed so exactly as in Egypt. They (the astrologers) have kept records in which these observations have been written down for an incredible number of years. Here one finds information on the relation of each planet to the birth of animals and on the good or bad influence of each star . . . At the tomb of Ozymandias in Thebes, there was a golden circle on the terrace, 365 cubits in circumference, which was divided into 365 parts, each part being a day of the year, and at the side had been written the natural rising and setting of the stars with the predictions which Egyptian astrologers drew from them.'

The zodiac of Dendera, a famous document which would merit a thorough study, is not the only evidence of Egyptian astrology which, in early times, was essentially focused on the person of the pharaoh. There is no evidence for individual horoscopes until later. But the magician is always mindful of the relation between his actions and the planetary dispositions. According to Spell 144 of the *Book of the Dead* he watches the position of the stars in the sky. He consults the books of astrology in silence and in secret. They are in fact accessible only to those who have been initiated for many years. In contrast to what we see today, astrology is not debased. It remains a temple science which is the exclusive province of experts and people of responsibility.

Thanks to their knowledge of astrological laws, the blessed travel the sky, the earth and the kingdom of the dead at will. The magician's spirit travels with them.

While observing the sky, he makes footprints in the soil seven

* Sadly, there is no serious study of this subject. There is abundant evidence, but it is very difficult to organise. We must wait a while longer for a work on Egyptian astrology based on hieroglyphic texts, signs of the zodiac and other celestial features. This will at last provide us with a true foundation for western astrology, which has been so distorted by the Greco-Roman tradition and most modern practices.

times. He recites the magic spells seven times in honour of the Thigh—the Great Bear—turning towards the north, the axis of the world.[14]

Knowledge of astrology is an essential aspect of the practice of magic. Familiarity with the stars is indispensable if one is to use the forces of the cosmos, to grasp the light and seize the moon in one's hand,[15] in other words, to master its influence rather than conquer it.

Closely Guarded Secrets and Ritual Requirements

'This,' states Spell 162 of the *Book of the Dead*, 'is a great secret. Let no one see it, that would be a shameful act. He who knows and guards the secret will continue to live. The name of this book is 'the sovereign of the hidden temple'.

These strictures, laid down for the attention of those who practise magic as rash laymen, do not deny the initiate access to the secrets. They demand silence only in the case of those who are ill-qualified or unskilled.

We know how this book and the secrets it contains were passed on to the magicians of Egypt. The god Thoth had assembled the masters of magic. The postulant had been received amongst them. He rinsed out his mouth, ate natron and proved that he was fit to join the Ennead, the group of nine powerful creators.[16] That means that he could successfully perform the tests from the beginning. The postulant, standing next to a master of magic who filled the role of the god Horus, wearing a mask in the shape of a falcon, had revealed to him words and formulas dating from the time when Osiris, the primordial ancestor, was still living and reigned over the land of Egypt.

The first test to verify that the postulant has truly understood all that has been entrusted to him, is for him to subdue a horned viper.

A cool head, knowledge of the sonorous spell which will hypnotise the reptile and a steady hand are all needed to deal with this: the future initiate is facing death.

The physical test passed, next comes the metaphysical revela-

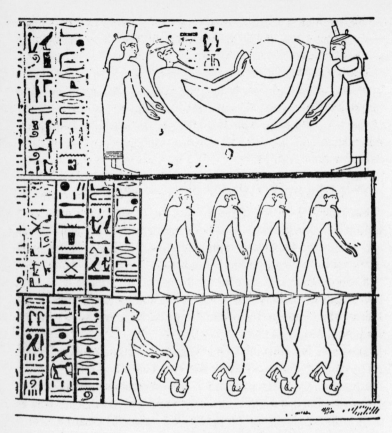

In the two lower registers are shown the two ways one can travel in the regions of the other world: either upright, or upside down. In the upper register, Isis and Nephthys support a semi-circular being who is magnetising a sun. The two great magicians in this way make the light of creation circulate in a curved universe. The Egyptians, in effect, saw the terrestrial surface (but not the earth) as flat and the cosmos as circular or curved.

tion. The masters of magic reveal to the initiate that the two gods who are so dissimilar and seem to be opposites, Re the radiant and Osiris the dark, are indeed one and the same. This one god was summoned under the name of the 'Reunited Soul', inside the House of Life. He was symbolised by a mummy wrapped in a ram's skin.[17] In contemplating this the new initiate is united with his own spirit and enters on the road to resurrection.

Only someone who is in a state of purity may gain knowledge of the secrets and of Unity. Anything discordant or detrimental to life is impure. Man is hampered by his own ties, he is not naturally transparent to life. Magic teaches him to free himself from the fetters with which he binds himself. External purity, the simple hygiene so prized by the priests of Egypt, is clear evidence of inner purity. The magician also washes himself frequently. When his mouth is purified, the words that come from it are pure also. Washing both hands and feet gets rid of harmful energies. 'Your feet were washed on a rock at the side of the lake of the god,' states Spell 172 of the *Book of the Dead*. This ritual act was considered sufficiently important to be carried out inside the temple. The king's feet were also washed as part of an imposing ceremony, and almost certainly it was this royal rite that inspired the scene in the Gospels, in which Christ stressed the importance of washing feet.

Once purified, the body is fit to receive a ritual vestment. Spell 117 of the *Book of the Dead* is specifically intended for the clothing in the *Wab* vestment, meaning 'the Pure', virtually a 'new body' of immaculate whiteness which the magician must be careful not to soil by deeds that threaten harmony.

On receiving the vestment, the initiate meditates and prays to the gods. He asks that he shall be delivered from impurity of body and soul. This tradition was preserved until the latest periods of the Egyptian civilisation: in a Greek Papyrus in the Bibliothèque Nationale (Paris) the magician is asked to dress himself in a vestment of fine linen, sing a hymn and recite a spell in the presence of a medium who stands before the sun.

Today as in former times, magic cannot be practised in any way one chooses or in any conditions. The requirements of the ritual are laid down in the *Book of the Heavenly Cow*,[18] which is written in columns of hieroglyphs in the Royal Tombs of the New Kingdom: 'For a man to pronounce this spell in the right way, he must be drenched in oil and ointments, with a censer filled with incense in his hand; he must have natron of one quality behind his ears, and natron of another quality in his mouth; he must be clothed in two new vestments, having washed in flood water, and be shod with white sandals, and have a picture of the goddess Maat (Universal Harmony) painted in fresh ink on his tongue.'

There are more details:[19] 'This spell must only be read when one is in a state of purity and without blemish, and has not eaten small animals or fish, and has not had carnal relations with a woman.'

Thus prepared and observing the strict rules, the magician is ready to trace the sacred sun design in which the forces he is manipulating write their names in the form of symbols. In 'the chamber of the two Maats' (that is, the two truths, cosmic and human), adorned in linen clothing, daubed with galena, duly purified, anointed with myrrh, shod in white sandals, the magician makes the offering of cattle, poultry, resin of terebinth, bread, beer and vegetables. Then he traces the ritual design according to what is laid down in the secret writings, onto a clean area of soil which has been covered with gypsum and has not been fouled by either pig or deer.[20] The builders of the Middle Ages did the same when they drew their 'lodge board' which in several contemporary Freemasons' initiation lodges is effectively recreated in each working session.

The magician is therefore essentially a Foreman appointed to devise a plan. He binds on his brow a 'scarf of knowledge' and utters the surprising declaration: 'My thoughts are the great magical incantations that come from my mouth.'[21]

Previously he has passed through a rite of resurrection in the course of which he lay on a reed mat, becoming a living mummy which, by magic, makes contact with the superior powers. The magician relives the sufferings of Osiris, risen again from the world of the dead.[22]

The Divine Tribunal, the Guardians of the Doors, the Ferryman

If a magician, on earth, recites the secret book on behalf of someone else, that man will not be flayed by the genies who always attack the evil-doer. He will not be beheaded, will not die beneath Seth's knife. will not be taken to any prison. Serenely he will enter the divine tribunal which awaits each being in the evening of his earthly life and will emerge again justified, and freed from the terror of injustice.[23]

This is one of the great services rendered by magic: to enable a just man to present himself before his judges with his head held high and without trembling. Certain Egyptologists, perhaps with a bad conscience, have accused the Egyptians of being 'tricksters'. They deceived the gods by abusing magic. There is actually a disarming naivety in this. It is the magic of knowledge which is on trial, not the 'tricks' of a fairground conjuror. Unless a man knows the laws of that magic, he is, in fact, disarmed and condemned in advance to a new material cycle, although that in no way implies reincarnation in the usual sense.

Other perils lie in wait for the initiate on his way to the other world. To pass through the four frontiers of the sky, the traveller must persuade the guardians to give him free passage. He must also recite the words of those who dwell in the secret places.[24] Many passages in the *Coffin Texts*[25] evoke these sinister personages who, often armed with knives and watching over lakes of unfathomed depths, are found on roads which are lost in shadows, and at crossroads where one may go astray. Only magic can destroy the power of these terrifying genies.

Another being demands magical skills of the highest order from the traveller in the Underworld. This is the ferryman who possesses the treasure of all treasures: the barque. It provides a means of crossing the expanses of water into the heavenly paradise. When the initiate asks to use the boat[26] the ferryman subjects him to a cross-examination: 'Who are you?' he asks him. 'I am a magician,' replies the initiate. He is 'whole, equipped, has power over all his limbs'. This declaration is judged inadequate. He must prove his qualifications as a magician by naming the different parts of the ferry and giving their mythological and esoteric equivalents. There is no way that the uninitiated layman can succeed, but the fully qualified magician will triumph. He will also govern the cities of the Netherworld, prepare an inventory of the wealth of the other world and will offer the poor what they need on earth. In other words, the social status of the magician is high; he is not only an 'intellectual' but also an administrator whose skills are used to help the underprivileged, even though this is a very strange form of economics.

The ferryman, however, is still not satisfied. He insists that the magician prove his mathematical skills by showing his ability to count on his fingers. Each finger, each 'numerical act', has a deep meaning.* This is not a question of ordinary mental arithmetic, but of the creation of the world by Numbers, not by figures.

Another question which the ferryman asks is, 'Where do you come from?' The answer is 'From the island of the flame', meaning, from the part of the universe where every morning the sun emerges victorious from his battle with the enemies of the light. Born of the sun, the magician has the temperament of a warrior and conqueror. He has proved it.

The essential fact is that the magician reveals to the ferryman that he has discovered the dockyard of the gods where the ferry lies aground, in separate pieces. Surely this is an analogy with the dismembered Osiris. But the magician knows how to rebuild it. He possesses the supreme art.

Overwhelmed by so much knowledge, the ferryman yields. He does what the magician asks of him, places the ferry at his disposal and returns to his post, where he waits to put the next traveller to the test.

Going Forth by Day

'He who understands the books of magic can go forth by day and walk on earth amongst the living. He will never die. This has proved possible, millions of times.'[27] We are surrounded by millions of Egyptian magicians, eternally alive. They have 'gone forth by day' because the power of magic is with them, enabling them to free themselves from everything that hampers their movements.[28] Doubtless, they are not always in human form but, as

---

* This very detailed 'counting' demands long study. In the author's opinion it is the still shadowy origin of the numerical Kabbala.

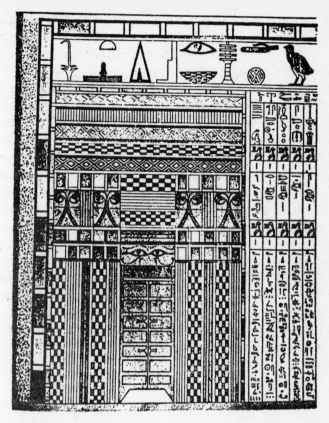

The hieroglyphic text (at the top) shows the offering which the king makes to Osiris. On the columns at the right are the names of those offerings. At the left, we see the door surmounted with the two eyes known as 'complete'. This is the door that separates the two worlds, ours and 'the other'. The 'dead man', when he finds himself in his tomb, can live for ever. If he has mastered the tests set by the Door, which is a living being, and its guardians, then he, in his turn, will show the way to those from the 'other side'.

Gerard de Nerval knew, hide themselves in stone, wood or metal.

'Going forth by day' is the daily ritual of the temples. In the morning when the priest opens the doors of the naos, the inner sanctuary, which contains the statue of the god, he speaks these words: 'The doors of the sky are open, the doors of the temple are unlocked. The house is open to its master. Let him go out when he wishes to go out, let him enter when he wishes to enter.'[29]

In the Underworld it is essential to walk on one's feet, not on one's head. The magic formulas save the initiate from this serious inconvenience and allow him to walk normally along the paths of the sky and the ground of the other world, as part of the retinue of the god Thoth.

The magician makes his way along the beautiful pathways of the West in the form of a being of light, having acquired, and experimented with, all the powers without becoming enslaved by them. He is identified with the young god born in the Beautiful West, who came from the land of the living, having shaken off the dust of the body, filled his heart with magic and slaked his thirst for knowledge. He turns towards the field of rushes which is one of the celestial paradises.[30] He comes and goes in the fields, towns and canals of the Netherworld. He tills the land, sees Re, Osiris and Thoth daily, has power over water and air, doing all he desires, such is the initiate of the Abbey of Thelame. Life is in his nose, he will not die, he lives in the field of offerings where his estates are settled for eternity. He has fulfilled his vow: to become a magician.[31]

3 The Powers of the Magician

The magician of Luxor and his sons were not at all surprised by the ancient texts of which I spoke. They found in them the echo of a centuries-old practice which had been passed down from generation to generation. Who could doubt a magician's immense powers, based on the depth of his knowledge? His only real fear, in this world or the other, is of being deprived of his magical skills by the intervention of some evil power. But he has at his disposal a special spell to ward off the danger: 'Not allowing a man's magic to be taken from him in the kingdom of the dead.'[1]

Having gained this assurance, he must do battle with the evil which tries constantly to strike at beings when they are at their lowest ebb. The magician, by referring to battles fought in the divine world, drives off harmful influences as the god Re saved himself from Sobek's dreadful crocodile, as Horus saved himself from his killer brother, Seth, as Thoth saved himself from the lustful Bebon.[2]

To fight evil, elaborate techniques are needed. The magician draws the harmful energy from the body of the affected person and transfers it elsewhere, into an animal for example. Sometimes it appears in male form and sometimes female. That is why the magician particularly distrusts ghosts and wandering spirits, which take many forms and are difficult to identify. He threatens to destroy the tombs from which they come so as to deprive them of their earthly 'base', or to remove their offerings so that they will die of hunger.

One can understand how the fame of the magicians of Egypt should be so widespread throughout the ancient world. According to the Greek and Roman authors, they knew how to heal the sick, use herbs, predict the future and even make rain fall.[3] Their actual magical powers were, alas, reduced to simple feats like giving a woman a superb head of hair which would not go white, or casting a spell upon an enemy to make him bald. The *Leyden Papyrus*[4] shows such a series of spectacular practices: divination, driving out evil spirits, making ointments, encouraging dreams, making a woman fall in love, attracting good fortune to oneself, blinding or killing one's enemies and using a spell to drive away the fear that cripples a man by night or day. All this rests upon foundations of traditions that have gradually been forgotten.

To prepare oneself for divination, a vase filled with water is used. Taking on the identity of ancient Horus, the great god of the cosmos, the magician questions the gods through a young medium who bears the truth within him. The magician orders him to open his eyes in order to see the light. He must at all costs keep the shadows away from the medium so that his spirit can penetrate the world of the gods and find there the answer to the question. The vase is an excellent aid to communication with heaven and the world between.

The magician is able to put himself to sleep, triggering a hypnotic sleep by placing himself in front of a light or by gazing at the moon, or even by reciting a magic spell seven times.

Amongst the official magical techniques, the oracle enjoyed great success in New Kingdom Egypt and in the Late Dynastic Period. The state magician puts questions to a divine statue from which he waits for an answer, which sometimes takes the form of a gesture when the sacred effigy bends its head to say either 'yes' or 'no'. In small oratories, 'private' clients consulted the divinities, either in writing or orally, about the everyday matters that preoccupy mankind—social advancement, the future, material goods, love.

It cannot be emphasised enough that each gain in magical power rests upon a process of identification which is abundantly illustrated in Egyptian texts. The magician 'becomes' the forces that created the world—for example, the personification of Abundance. The beneficial results of his art are not for his own personal benefit but for the benefit of a patient.

Magic in the Temples and in the Towns

Magic is everywhere in the temples—in the practice of the rituals, in the very meaning of the architecture and sculpture, but also because, amazing as it may seem, the images carved upon the walls are alive, living. They come to life when the ritual words are spoken. During the morning ceremony, the most important of the day, the image of the pharaoh, at the same moment in all the temples of Egypt, 'comes down' from the wall where it is engraved and becomes incarnate in the body of the priest who represents him.

According to a stela of the reign of Rameses IV, the temples are themselves magically protected by amulets and spells so that all evil is driven from their body. Body is the most appropriate word, since each sanctuary is looked upon as a living being.

Whatever is within the temples (stelae, reliefs, furniture, etc.) as in the tombs, must be preserved by magic. Anyone who raises his hand against these objects or against the administrative decrees recorded upon the walls of the monuments will perish beneath the sword of Amun or the fire of Sekhmet, the lion-goddess.

The towns, like the temples, enjoyed magical protection. The conurbation of Thebes is a typical example.[5] Thebes, Hermontis, Medamud and Tod were the four sanctuaries of the god Montu. The one at Medamud housed four statues, the centre of magic for the whole region. A text explains that 'Amon-Re, chief of the gods, is in the middle of the right Eye, complete in its parts . . . whatever Thebes is that is Medamud also: the Eye, complete in its parts because His Majesty, Amon-Re, is one of the five gods who founded Thebes as a complete Right Eye. The four Montu guard it. They come together in that town to repel the enemy of Thebes.' The Montu, warrior gods, have the role of protecting Thebes, ever watchful against her enemies, both visible and invisible. Thebes is seen, in effect, as the complete and healthy Eye, *wedjat*, often found as an amulet. The plan of the temples of the Theban area, in particular that of Medamud, embodies this cosmic Eye, the major key to Egyptian symbolism.

Let us not forget that the sign of the Eye, in hieroglyphs, signifies 'to make, to create'.

There is also a spell for the protection of the family home and its elements, the window, the bolts, the bedchamber, the bed . . . Each part of the house is assigned to a special protectress, a female falcon, Ptah, chief artisan, 'he whose name is hidden' and other spirits. Thus, enemies will not enter either by day or by night.[6]

Conquering Death

The magician is a 'specialist' in life as in death. When the soul leaves the body, all is scattered. The constituent parts of the being, until then associated with the phenomenon of 'life', no longer live together. Thus death is a very dangerous transition, for the different elements run the risk of remaining separate on the other side of the mirror. This then is the 'second death', the ultimate extinction of the individual. Hence the need for magic: to preserve the unity of the being during its passage from this world to the other and make it live again on the other side in its fulness.

Mummification is a magical act. Particular care is taken to conserve the viscera in special vases, canopic jars. Each jar is placed under the protection of a divinity, one of the four 'Sons of Horus'. Imseti, who has a man's head, protects the liver, Hapi, baboon-headed, the kidneys, Duamutef, who has the head of a dog, the stomach, and falcon-headed Kebehsenuef the intestines. It is not only the physical organs that benefit from divine favour but also the subtle principles which they house. The being, according to Egyptian esoterism, is composed of various 'qualities' of which the best known are the *akh*, the radiant light, the *ba*, the power of incarnation and the *ka*, the vital power. There is also the *heka*, the individual's capacity for magic.* Each

---

* The *akh* is symbolised by an ibis. In the beginning, it is the supernatural power of the gods and the king. The *ba* is the individual's faculty of movement, represented by a bird with a human head. The *bau* (the Egyptian plural of the term) of the towns are their supernatural power, their particular genius. The *ka* is Force. The *ka* of food, for example, is its energising properties. As sexual power, the *ka* is animation of matter.

element has an independent existence. The magician's art lies in making all of them pass through the openings of the sky, so that the complete being may come and go, and make its way to the light.[7]

In the extraordinary words of the *Pyramid Texts*,[8] the dead did not leave dead, but living. This statement applies to the king and the initiates who are regenerated by the rites. The purpose of funerary magic is to provide renewed life which needs the perfect functioning of the heart-conscience, the vital organs, free movement in the heavenly realms and the enjoyment of the subtle energies contained in the food and drink served at the banquets of the Netherworld.[9]

If a magician was not a master of his art, that would be a cosmic catastrophe. The sun would not rise, the sky would be deprived of the gods, the order of the world would be overturned, the rites would not be celebrated, the rhythm of everything would be disturbed.[10] As master of energy, the magician empowers the forces of light to display their full power. One of their names most often used is 'powers of Heliopolis', the sun city. They engender prosperity. When energy is unbalanced, the powers are no longer revealed. Children are no longer born.[11]

The preservation and transmission of life are magical deeds, by which apparently inert bodies are brought to life. For example, a statue appears to be nothing but a stone object. By the rite of 'the opening of the mouth' the statue is brought to life. A spiritual presence inhabits it. In the mastabas, the tombs of the Old Kingdom, the *serdab*, a small enclosed room, houses a statue—alive— of the deceased. His *ka* is present in that statue. It profits from the recitation of spells which will give it the energy it needs.

The famous 'models' which were placed in the tombs are not toys, but magical objects. For example, the little wooden boats with their oarsmen become in the Netherworld the very real means of transport which give the traveller the power to sail upon the eternal waters of the cosmos.

Life is threatened by hostile forces, especially by souls which have escaped from their tombs because of mistakes in magic or inadequately performed rituals. They wander, causing serious

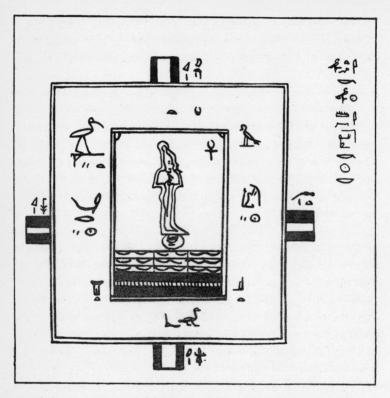

A symbolic representation of the House of Life where magicians learn their art. The square is bounded by the four cardinal points. In the inner enclosure is the figure of Osiris whose secret name is given by the hieroglyph at the top right: 'Life'. The aim of the initiates of the House of Life was no less than that of ritually and magically creating Life.

physical and psychical damage. It is the task of the magician, who learns the secrets of the invisible world in the House of Life, to neutralise them. To the man who knows the statue named 'Life' which is at the heart of that school of initiates, it is said, 'You will be sheltered from sudden death, you will be sheltered from fire, you will be sheltered from the sky, it will not fall on you and the earth will not overturn, and Re will not make cinders with the gods and goddesses.'[12] This statuette 'Life' is mummified, then covered with coats of ointment and with a substance called 'divine stone' and finally laid in a coffin. It is consecrated before its mouth is opened and is placed in a ram-skin, a 'Skin of resurrection'. The 'Life', thus protected, is kept in a tent of the House of Life where it is constantly renewed by the rites.[13]

Symbolically, the House of Life is a sandy courtyard surrounded by a wall pierced by four gates. Inside a tent is erected to house a reliquary containing a mummy of Osiris. All around are other buildings, houses, shops and workshops where the specialists hired to carry out the rituals are trained. In Egypt the magic of the rites is not just a meaningless expression. It actually gives life and conquers death. The magician spreads amulets on the mummy, with accompanying gestures, so making the 'dead' pass from his human to his divine body. The bandages that wrap the mummy are the concern of a goddess, Tait, whose role is to keep the body from decomposing. Tait is also the goddess who creates the royal vestments.[14] In other words, she confers royal rank upon an individual who has been ritually mummified.

The opening of the mouth and of the eyes are acts that transform the cadaver into a living being. The magician uses an adze to open the mouth, fumigates it by placing incense in a flame, and purifies it with the water of youth.[15] Ptah, the father of the gods, is asked to bless the opening of the mouth and eyes as he did for the god Sokaris in the workshop of the sculptors of Memphis called 'the Mansion of Gold'.[16] One of the most beautiful illustrations of the rite is found in the tomb of Tutankhamun where the king Ay, clad in a panther skin, opens the mouth of the young dead king, represented as Osiris.

The important point is that the sarcophagus is not a tomb nor an enclosed place. It is seen as a ship and as the belly of the sky. In the Middle Kingdom, false doors were painted on the exterior walls and two eyes at the height of the mummy's eyes. The spirit of the 'dead' man enters the sarcophagus and leaves it. The tomb, likewise, is a place of passage. The false door, at first placed in the middle of the east side of the mastaba, allows communication between this world and the next. The spirit passes through matter.

The Name, Key to Magic Power

Knowledge of the name is true power. To pronounce the name is to fashion a spiritual image, to reveal the essence of a being. By naming, one creates. By knowing the true names which are hidden from the uninitiated, mastery is achieved.

The worst fate for any being is to see his name destroyed. Magic therefore takes every precaution to ensure that the name lasts for ever.[17] The elements of the name, the letters that form it, carry energy. When the magician speaks ritually he uses these sounds like living matter, works upon the exterior world and modifies it if necessary.

Every being—even the gods—possesses a secret name. The sun-god, Re, is no exception to this rule. His father and mother gave him his true name, which was hidden at his birth.[18] Some secret names are revealed by the texts in the course of rather odd episodes. For example, Horus was sailing with his brother in a golden ship. The latter was bitten by a serpent. He appealed to Horus for help. The god said, 'Reveal your name to me.' It is only on that condition that Horus, the doctor, will summon up the great god to begin the process of healing. In the circumstances, his brother is obliged to give way. He admits: 'I am yesterday, today and tomorrow,' 'I am a man of a million cubits in height whose nature is unknown,' 'I am a giant' ... Horus hears this litany but remains sceptical. The true name does not appear amongst these. The other yields. Finally sincere, he gives his secret name: 'The day when a woman gave birth to a son.'[19] Horus pronounces the healing spell. We must surely see in this tale a symbolic representation of the hermaphrodite, that male-female being who existed at the dawn of time before the spirit was divided into 'male' and 'female'.

The most famous example of the search for the secret name is offered by the legend of Isis and Re. The goddess was determined to discover the true name of the god of light. She had just one weapon which would serve her ends: magic. When Re grew very old his saliva dribbled onto the earth. Isis used this precious substance. She moulded it in her hand with the earth that clung to it. With this paste she made a serpent which she placed on a path along which Re passed. Poorly protected by his followers, the sun god was stung by the reptile. Absolutely amazed, Re cries to the heavens. 'What is happening?' wonders the lord of the light. He trembles, he stutters. The poison circulates in his veins and takes possession of his body. He calls the gods. They appear before him, the issue of his being. Re explains that he has been bitten by a harmful creature. He didn't see it and doesn't know what it is. It is not of his making and he has no control over it. Re suffers terribly, he has never felt such pain. He speaks the words which every magician repeats when he identifies himself with the god: 'I am a Great One, son of a great one, I am a seed which is born of a god. I am a great magician, son of a great magician . . . I have many names and many forms, my form is in each god.'

Re unbosoms himself. His father and mother gave him a name which has remained secret in the depth of his being. That is why no magician or sorceress has any power over him. But he has been touched by an evil which he does not recognise even though he is walking on the earth which he created. What is this unbearable pain? It comes from neither fire not water. His body trembles, he begins to feel cold.

'Bring the children of the gods,' he orders, 'those who can speak the words that will help, those whose mouths are wise, whose skill reaches to heaven.' Everyone makes haste, everyone tries to help Re.

One goddess was famous for her exceptional magical gifts and her ability to give the breath of life, bringing back to life one who was no longer breathing: Isis. She comes and asks Re, 'What is happening? What does this mean?' She is told that a serpent has bitten Re. Will she therefore drive out the venom with an appropriate spell?

Re's condition worsens. He is colder than water, hotter than fire. His limbs are covered in sweat. He can no longer see.

Isis approaches him. Catlike she murmurs, 'Tell me your name, divine father.' Does she not need it to formulate the spell that will enable Re to stay alive? The god replies, 'I am he who made the heaven and the earth, established the mountains and created that which is above.' He adds that he brought into existence the elements and the horizons, and put the gods in the sky. When he opens his eyes the light is born. When he closes them, there is darkness. He generates fire, the days, the years, the flowers. But his name remains unknown. It is known that he calls himself Khepri in the morning, Re at noon, Atum in the evening . . . But that will not be enough to drive out the poison. The great god is not healed.

Isis confirms this. 'Your secret name is not among those you have told me. Confess it to me and the poison will go.' Re's condition worsens still more. 'Lend me your ear, my daughter,' he says to Isis, 'so that my name may pass from my bosom to yours.'

Thus Re reveals his secret name to Isis. Unfortunately, the hearing of humans was not sharp enough to catch the words which the god spoke. Only the goddess was in his confidence. To know the secret, to hear the lost word, one must be initiated into her mysteries.

Each human being has the task of seeking for the secret name which was entrusted to him at birth and which he needs to make him worthy. To pass the test of death victoriously is to make that name permanent like that of Osiris. The importance of the name is such that it is taken into account, valued as sacred by the tribunals. Thus, the names of criminals who have violated a holy place or tried to build a home higher than that of the gods, are changed. The first level of punishment is to remove from the name of the accused that of the god who might have been part of it. In the plot against Rameses III, the criminals used magic to assassinate the king. So their names were changed to make them odious: henceforth they would be called 'Re hates him', 'Evil in Thebes', 'the demon'. These awful names were a punishment in themselves. One could go further and suppress all memory of the guilty man by making it disappear, for the name is an essential component of survival. The dead man without a name is condemned to second death. He is destroyed to the depth of his being.[20]

In the kingdom of the dead, everyone must remember their name.[21] The magician presents himself as a builder who deserves a pre-eminent place in the sky. His name has been spoken in the temples. He remembered in the night to count the years and the months, during his initiation into the mysteries when he was recognised by his peers as proficient. To the gods, he states explicitly that his name is a god who dwells in his body.[22] To the Eternal Stars whom he meets in the sky, he declares, 'I know your names.'[23]

But the 'true name' of the gods is never spoken in the presence of the uninitiated. Sometimes they pretend to reveal it by reciting a stream of incomprehensible sounds that mean nothing. Thus the initiates of the House of Life discourage the curious who wish to acquire power for themselves rather than to decipher the deep meaning of the hieroglyphs. Each divine name is actually formed from consonants which give the esoteric significance of each divine personality. Let us take an example. The name of the jackal-god, Anubis, is made up of an *i*, an *n* and a *p* which gives *inp*, hence, with the addition of vowels to make it pronounceable, Anubis (*a* for *i*, which is a semi-consonant in Egyptian, *b* being interchangeable with *p*). Now the *Papyrus Jumilhac* explains clearly that each letter that makes up the name of Anubis has a precise meaning. Through them, the god has power over the breath of life, energy and matter, three qualifications indispensable to his role as embalmer, initiator and master of the ceremonies during the rites of resurrection.

Knowledge of the secret names gives access to the celestial paradises[24] whose gates are opened by Re and by Nut. At each gate to the Netherworld, the magician must prove that he knows the name of the guardian and of the gate itself. He must give details. The guardian of the threshold, Anubis, asks the one who wishes to enter, 'Do you know the names of the threshold and the lintel?' He must reply, 'Master of rectitude who is on his two legs' (name of the lintel) and 'master of force, who lets in the cattle' (name of the threshold). As in all brotherhoods of initiates, the traveller is tested.[25] If his knowledge is enough, they say to him, 'Pass, for you know!'

He must still avoid the fishermen who catch the souls of the dead in their nets. To achieve this the magician shows that he knows the occult name of each part of the net from which he, therefore, has nothing to fear.[26]

Born on the soil of Egypt, Christianity has not forgotten the magic of the name. The Coptic magician identifies himself with Christ, and with Mary, commands the gods, the spirits and the angels, threatens the devil, prays, all by evoking the 'true names' by which he hopes to become fully effective.

4 The Tools of Magic

Amulets

Both living and dead enjoy the protection of amulets which they wear about their person. These often represent the great gods (Re, Horus, Osiris) who guarantee an excellent journey through the skies, safety, health and other such good fortune. An amulet is 'inscribed' on various media, papyrus or linen, for example. It is knotted, rolled, suspended by a cord around the neck; the important thing is that it should be in contact with the person.

When the magician creates an amulet, he puts into an object the forces which are essential to the preservation of life and to guarantee the immunity of a body or a mummy; to protect the latter completely one hundred and four amulets are needed. Attached either to the big toes or the feet, they make the magic power circulate throughout the body before reaching the head.[1] They give protection from evil in all its forms.

That is why a good mother has an extensive knowledge of amulets which she uses to shield her child from outside perils. And do they not also promote love, vitality and success at work?

Gold, bronze, glass, faience and stone are used in the making of amulets. The *Leyden Magical Papyrus* describes the method for preparing a top-quality talisman: take a linen band with sixteen threads (four white, four green, four blue, four red), dye them with the blood of a hoopoe and tie them to a scarab in the form of the sun god clothed in the finest linen. Thus the whole religious universe of ancient Egypt is revealed in the little world of amulets: one sees here a pleiad of deities, sacred animals, the royal trap-

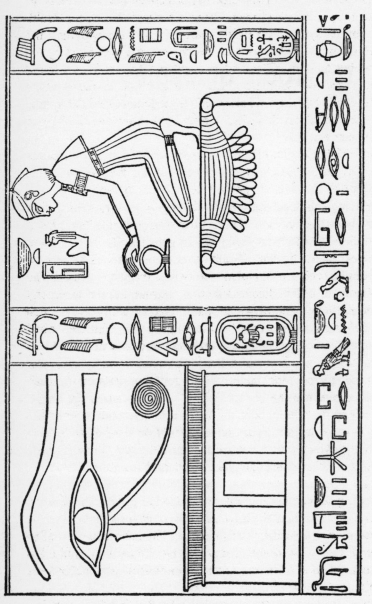

Some of the magic symbols used in amulets: on the left, the wedjat eye, the 'complete' and perfect eye which gives the initiate a total vision of reality; on the right, Nephthys, whose name signifies 'the ruler of the Temple' gives power to the sign chen whose magical protection guards its possessor from being 'torn apart' by negative forces. She is seated on the sign for gold, from which the flesh of the god is made.

pings (such as the royal crowns) which confer the status of
pharaoh upon the dead man, abstract concepts like Life, Health
and Power (symbolised by the 'key of Life', the papyrus), the
heart, the transfiguration of the incarnate being incarnated by the
scarab beetle, stability by a pillar. Ordinary objects have profound
significance: the staircase allows one to climb to the sky, the
bedhead grants a reviving sleep safe from demons, builder's tools
(drawing board, level, square, plumb-bob) show how the Master
Craftsmen worked.

As is the rule with magic, it is the Word which gives amulets
their Essence. Thus chapters 155–160 of the *Book of the Dead*
are entitled: 'Words to pronounce upon a *djed*-pillar of gold
placed upon the neck of the blessed, upon a knot of red jasper
placed upon the neck of the blessed, upon a golden vulture placed
upon the neck of the blessed, upon a golden collar placed upon
the neck of the blessed'. The blessed is, in effect, the one who
is endowed with such an assurance against the forces of evil. The
djed-pillar merits particular attention. During a grand ceremony
connected with State magic, pharaoh re-erected this pillar which
was lying on the ground. In this way he recreated the spinal
column of the kingdom. This column is in effect the secret axis
of the body of Osiris. It makes the State stable because it conforms
to the divine. Over the *djed*-pillar this spell is recited: 'Your back
is yours, you who have a quiet heart, your vertebrae are yours,
you who have a quiet heart. You sleep on your side worn out, I
pour water over you. See, I have brought the *djed*-pillar, so that
you may take pleasure in it.'[2] An enigmatic spell, whose purpose
is to see a being stand again, take up an axis, and gain the stability
needed to endure.

Having spoken these words the magician places the pillar on
a clay brick. A niche is prepared for it in the western wall of the
tomb and it is turned towards the east. Then the niche is walled
up with earth mixed with cedar oil. The pillar is invisible, but
present. Thanks to it, the tomb is immutable and becomes a
dwelling of eternity.[3]

Some amulets are surprising, such as the 'hand of Atum', a
goddess who drove the tempest from the sky and who reminds

us of the primordial masturbation of the creator. This hand, called 'Powerful', helps the light to banish the demon of darkness. She drives away suffering and impurity.[4] It is also she who, in the absence of the mother or nurse, places an amulet in a child's hand to protect it. She is none other than 'the hand of Isis' who watches over her son Horus and ensures his health and well-being.[5]

The frog—really the goddess Heket—is an amulet which favours resurrection,[6] because of her own birth in the silt of the Nile. The strangest creatures decorate amulets: such as pateques, nude and deformed figures, with shaven heads, sometimes children, sometimes adults,[7] whose role is to drive away demons.

The important point is that amulets are as effective for the living as for the dead. How can one guarantee one's vital functions, either here on earth or in the hereafter, without the intelligent use of amulets? Through them, the fortunate man has the chance to join the servants of Horus, the ruler of the world of the stars.[8]

In the Late Period amulets proliferated on the wave of popular magic which became more and more naive and farther and farther from its source. The power of the hair of cattle or even goats and other such unappetising substances was shortsightedly used to make talismens. This is just a caricature of magic.

Gold and Precious Stones

It was Re's influence that caused gold to be put upon the flesh of the dead to give it its glowing colour. How better to show that the just man has attained everlasting life?[9] At the end of a correctly conducted mummification, the magician confirms the transmutation and exclaims, 'O undead! You have just received your golden fingerstalls and your fingers are covered with gold, your nails with electrum! The radiation of Light reaches you, she who is truly the divine body of Osiris. Gold will illumine your face in the world between, you will breathe because of gold, you will come forth because of gold.'[10]

Gold is the sign of life reborn. The great magician, Isis, takes care that the initiate renews his life by means of the gold he has discovered within him. His face is therefore radiant with joy. He appears as a 'young boy reborn'.[11] These texts, on the evidence, refer to an initiation of an alchemic sort.

In the resurrection scene in the tomb of Petosiris at Hermopolis, the god of the underworld, Osiris, has become the sun god. Radiating gold, he sheds living light. The initiates of the mysteries of Thoth reveal to us that Osiris is inseparable from Re from whom issued a stone and a gum which were intended to render incorruptible the mummy of the deceased, who is identified with Osiris.

This stone of light is assuredly the prototype of the alchemists' philosopher's stone.*

Knots and Numbers

The Egyptian magician spends a large part of his time tying knots. A magic knot is a point of convergence of the forces which unite the divine and the human worlds. Spells 406–408 of the *Coffin Texts* are spells for knowing the seven knots of the heavenly cow. They will be useful to the magician in manoeuvring the ferry in which he crosses the expanses of heaven. They restore the body to health and vigour. Moreover the heavenly knots find their equivalents in the 'knots' of the human body, those sensitive points where the streams of energy meet, upon which our existence depends.

Some spells, such as those of the *London and Leyden papyrus*,[13] give us valuable techniques. They turn upon the number or the colour. A knot tied on earth is also tied in heaven and vice versa. Christ makes use of this symbolic idea which is traceable in the Coptic magical papyri. 'Let my voice reach you,' declares the magician to the powers, 'you who untie the cords, the knots and the chains so that you may untie all chains for ever.'

* The origin of precious stones used for magical purposes is described thus: 'Precious stones come for you, they float on the wave for you from the interior of the mountains, making themselves the protectors of the thickets of papyrus, at the leaves of the first door of the necropolis.'[12]

The magic of numbers is inseparable from that of knots. A number is considered to be an abstract knot. We still lack a thorough study of the symbolism of numbers in ancient Egypt. However, they are there all the time, even in the State magic. One of the best examples is that of an altar of the cult of Heliopolis, an offering table made of four tables joined together[14] upon which are placed loaves that serve to mark the four compass points of space, the 'four orientation points'. In other words, the cosmos is organised on the basis of a central unity which alone can give reality to what is offered to the gods. In Heliopolis' cosmic religion, four was the number of usefulness, reality and efficacy.

Seven is without doubt the most frequently quoted number. Cords with seven knots, seven rings of stone and gold, seven linen threads ... one would need a litany of examples. The *Leyden Magical Papyrus*[15] quotes a ritual in which Seven is used throughout. Choose seven unused bricks. Handle them without letting them touch the earth and place them according to the ritual, being yourself in a state of purity. Three serve to support a receptacle containing oil, the other four are placed about a medium. Then bring seven pure loaves of bread, seven blocks of salt, and a plate freshly filled with oil from the oases. All these are placed around the receptacle of oil. The magician makes the medium lie down on his belly. He chants an incantation while the medium stares at the oil, seven times. At the seventh hour of the day ask any question you wish.

The Substitute Body

There is plenty of evidence in the magical practices of ancient Egypt about the substitute body, often call a 'golem' in the practices of the Kabbala. This body, also called 'subsidiary', is seen not only in the voodoo figurines but also in many royal and private statues. It is not only the replacement bodies which are animated and filled with life, but also the wooden models representing servants, workmen and soldiers which were placed in the tomb to live there eternally in the fullness of their youth, fulfilling their purpose.

In the case of waxen images, we are talking of a substitute body upon which are unleashed aggressive forces, under the magician's control.[16] Shabtis, whose name means 'those who answer' (to the dead's call for help) are, on the other hand, vehicles for positive energies. These are little figures of wood, faience or bronze which carry two hoes. Their bodies are covered with a magic text. They carry a bag which hangs on their back. They serve as magical substitutes for a just man, going to work, at his request, in the fields of the Netherworld. In the Middle Kingdom, when these shabtis first appeared, there was usually only one in the tomb. Then their number increased rapidly. In the Late Period the chests often contained more than five hundred shabtis. These figurines are always associated with the sixth chapter of the *Book of the Dead*.[17] It gives a spell which obliges the shabti to obey. He is charged with the most arduous tasks: he cultivates the fields, sees to the irrigation of the banks, and transports the silt to fertilise the land. To every request of the magician he replies, 'Here I am.' The predecessor of the spell in the *Book of the Dead* appears in the *Coffin Texts*[18] in which it is said that the initiate has assumed his power before the gods, the spirits and the dead. He occupies their thrones. Unpleasant tasks are not inflicted upon him.

To be effective, this magic spell must be pronounced over an image of the figurine's owner, while he is still of this world, an image made of tamarisk or zizyphus wood which will be placed in the mortuary chapel.

Letters to the Dead

The Egyptians did not consider 'life' and 'death' as separated by an insuperable barrier. The spirits of those who are called 'dead' are travelling. They are not cut off from the living, towards whom they are sometimes benevolent and sometimes malevolent. We can communicate with these beings of the other world by various means, especially in writing.[19]

These letters to the dead are most often written on a bowl. If the inscription is very long, papyrus or cloth are used. In the beginning the bowls were cult objects in which bread or grain was placed. The Egyptians thought that, persuaded by a well argued letter, a dead person would intervene in the fate of the living, either for good or ill. He who challenges a dead man risks the chastisement of the divine tribunal. He who defaces a tomb will have his neck broken like that of a bird. He who does not enter a tomb in a state of purity will see himself plagued by all manner of ills. All this proves that the dead are present in our daily lives. Why not ask them to resolve or try to resolve problems as complicated as 'disputes over inheritance'? Thus a dead mother is asked to act as arbiter between her two sons.

Amongst the letters to the dead, one is particularly famous. It is a missive addressed by an unhappy husband to his dead wife. The document was attached to a statue of a woman, made of wood covered with plaster and coloured, an excellent magical medium for sending the letter to its recipient.[20]

In their life, husband and wife were a happy and fortunate couple, living in Memphis at the end of the New Kingdom. The wife died from an incurable illness. Her husband spent eight months in deep mourning, scarcely eating or drinking, crying without cease at the tomb of the one he loved. For three years his sorrow did not lessen. But he felt himself bewitched. He therefore wrote a letter of protest to his wife: 'What evil have you wrought to bring me to this painful state in which I find myself? What have I done to you to justify your laying hands on me, when I have committed no unkindness against you? . . . I accuse you through these words, before the Ennead who are in the West, and judgement will be passed on you and upon this letter which contains the facts of this affair. What have I done that you should act thus?'

History does not record what came of this plea to a dead woman. However, this extraordinary document shows that the psychic universe of the ancient Egyptians was open to all forms of reality.

The Lamp

The *Leyden Papyrus*[21] confers a particular magic role upon the lamp since it is one of the key elements of a method of divination. In a dark room a hole is dug out of the east wall. The magician takes a white lamp. He fills it with virgin oil from the oases. He recites the prayers of adoration to Re, as the sun rises. He lights the lamp, being in a state of purity. A medium enters with her eyes closed. The magician puts his finger on her head. Incense burns in a brazier. The magician asks the medium to open her eyes and look at the lamp. He sees the shadow of a divinity near her. It is the latter who answers the magician's questions about the matters that concern him.

The magician must take a new lamp with a clean wick. He writes hieroglyphs and symbols on the wick, places the lamp on

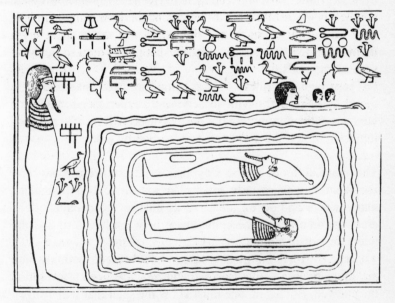

Magical rituals for making the initiate pass from the mortal body into the risen body. The magic power is symbolised by a wavy line ending in human head and arms. This is the fluid which wakens the bodies laid out in the protective ovals. The magic of resurrection is seen here as a true knowledge of the power.

a brick in front of him. He casts the spells, seeking to see the deity who shows herself on the lamp so that questions may be asked. The divinity presents herself under many names. She gives light, being the friend of the flame, the divine presence within the fire. The magician demands that she reveal herself, that very night, and speak with him, to speak the truth to him without lying.

To practise this kind of divination it is necessary to anoint the eyes with an unguent made with the flowers of the Greek bean as the prime ingredient. Having first cooked them, the magician places them in a glass vase and seals it, putting it in a dark and secret place for twenty days. If it is opened, a phallus and pair of testicles are found. Forty days later, the phallus has become bloody. It must then be placed in a glass receptacle within a pot which is itself put in a secret place. The magician must fill his eyes with the blood duly collected. Whilst chanting the spells, he stretches out on a mat of reeds, having been chaste in the days that went before: he addresses the lamp, the witness of the divine world, which has travelled in space and received the message of the gods.

These complex rituals, which belong to a late magic, mingle the primordial myths with sorcery. Only experienced magicians were capable of extracting the positive aspects from this mumbo-jumbo in which the good and bad lie side by side.

The magical tools of the Egyptian magician were many and various. They were only tools. The substitute body, amulets, magic knots and so on all serve as aids to the magician. The creative force lies in the communion between his spirit and the universe, not in simple objects.

Certainly, there are objects said to be 'charged', within which are more or less active traces of the magical works for which they served. But again, one must know the spell that will awaken that hidden energy. How can one achieve that without mastering the elemental powers?

5 Mastery of the Elements

Mastery of earth will not be covered in this chapter because of a remark of my host at Luxor. 'The earth,' he told me, 'belongs to the serpents and scorpions. She is our mother, but a demanding and dangerous one. The magician is no fool. To understand the treasures of the earth, one must first gain the friendship of those who defend her. But that is impossible for one who is not a man of water, air and fire.'

Strange words, which nevertheless would not surprise an ancient Egyptian used to living in harmony with the elements. They did not regard them with indifference. They knew that they held part of the secret of their own lives.

Water and the Barque

All water comes from Nun, the primeval ocean which surrounds the world. Each evening the sun enters Nun anew, regenerates itself there and emerges in the morning purified and renewed. The sacred lakes of the temples contain precisely that same primordial water in which the priests purify themselves.

The *Pyramid Texts* give a magic spell for gaining mastery over water.[1] It says that the celestial Nile is at the disposal of the magician who takes on the identity of the great god whose name is not known to the spirits of the wave. He speaks these words: 'O Hapy, prince of the sky, refresh my heart with your running water! Give me power over water ... Give me the water that existed before the gods, because I came into existence on the first day.'[2] To be sure of success, the magician transforms himself into the Nile-god, lord of the waters which enable plants to grow. That is why his magic remains on heaven and earth.[3]

The magician bathes with Re in the expanses of the heavenly waters. He is surrounded by Orion, Sothis and the morning star. They place him in the arms of his mother Nut, the sky. He also escapes the wrath of the damned who hang their heads as they walk.[4]

Purifying water, water for bathing in, but also water which serves to support the movements of the cosmos. According to the oldest religious texts, pharaoh sailed on rafts of reeds in the heavenly void. Every magician, following the example of the king, wishes 'to climb to the sky, embark on the ship of Re and become a living god'.[5] The magician can use a vase to see the barque of the sun. He asks the mother of the gods to open the sky to him, where he will see the divine barques go up and down.[6]

The magic spells are spoken over a barque of Re painted white and placed in a pure place.[7] Before it is the image of a blessed one. The magician draws a barque of the night on his right and a barque of the day on his left. Chapter 133 of the *Book of the Dead* gives a detailed explanation: 'Words to be spoken over a barque four cubits long, painted with green powder and having on it the divine assembly of nomes; make a starry sky, purified with natron and terebinth resin. Then trace an image of Re in white on a new bowl which will be placed before this barque and put the image of the blessed one whom you wish to glorify in this barque: he is allowed to sail in Re's barque.'

The magician who gains power over the celestial water becomes the paddle of Re which neither gets wet in a liquid nor is burnt by the fire.[8] By becoming identified with this paddle, the magician cannot fail to 'steer his barque'.

He is confronted by water in a much more direct and risky way when he is obliged to swim. There is an appropriate technique: To protect the swimmer and keep him from all danger, pay homage to a baboon, seven cubits tall, with eyes of electrum, lips of fire, whose every word is a flame.[9]

The body contains water. It is indispensable to life. To drink is a sacred act. The magician has at his disposal the water which comes from Elephantine, from Nun itself. He can take on the identity of the father of the gods.[10] There is a spell, 'to drink water in the kingdom of the dead', which contains this appeal: 'Come to me each day, you who are the water of rejuvenation! Refresh my heart with the fresh water of your stream! Grant that I may have power over water like She who is Powerful!' This miraculous water will be offered to the magician whose spirit is found at the beginning of time.[11]

'Fresh Water' is one of the names of the rejuvenated magician who knows the joy of living, of moving at will, of being protected

The king pours out water before one of the forms of the sun god. This 'water' is polarised energy (the double wave) needed to feed the ball of fire which manifests itself in the solar disc and from which comes the water of life.

and appearing in glory. Nut, the goddess of the sky, and Nephthys, the mistress of the temple, come to bring him the Eye of Horus, the measure of all things.[12] The initiate greets Re.[13] He demands that the god brings him the milk of Isis, the wave of Nephthys, the flooding of the sea, life, prosperity, health, happiness, bread, beer, clothing and nourishment: in brief, all those liquid forms which bring perfect happiness. He hopes to see Re when he comes forth as Thoth, when a watery way is prepared for the sun's barque.

The magician assumes the identity of Osiris. Now, Osiris made a long journey—as a corpse—in the waters. The Eye of Horus is beside him as he floats. The scarab Kheper hovers over him. The magician must protect the god from the harmful creatures that lurk in the waters. He must secure the help of the gods who are there in their boats.[14] There is also a spell to free waters which are filled with demons: 'Osiris is on the water, the Eye of Horus is with him. The great scarab stretches over him. Do not look up, dwellers in the waters, so that Osiris may pass above you.'[15]

The Nile harbours dangerous and malevolent creatures which attack both animals and humans who cross the river. They must not be allowed to do so. The magician recites songs, the 'water-charms'.[16] The words of these charms are ultra-secret. On this matter he is advised: 'Do not reveal them to the common man. This is a mystery of the House of Life.' A few hints let us into part of the secret. The magician uses an egg which is 'great in the sky and in the *Duat* (the world between earth and sky)'. A little bird hatches from it. The magician leaves the nest with it. The magic words must be spoken over a clay egg which represents the primordial egg. Taking it in his hand, the magician sits in the prow of the boat as it floats on the river. If a harmful creature breaks the surface and threatens to attack, the magician throws the egg in the water. The danger is thus averted.

The 'water-charms' tend to be very long and complicated for danger threatens the traveller and herdsman frequently and very directly. The magician therefore becomes very solemn in his pronouncements:[17] 'O ancient one who rejuvenates himself in his due time, aged one who becomes young! Let Thoth come to my call! Behind me is he who lives in the water; if the one on the water is attacked so will the Eye of Horus be also! (in other words, the order of the world will be compromised). Let not the one in the water raise his head before Osiris has passed!'

Even Re takes precautions when he travels by boat to visit the Ennead. The 'masters of the *Duat*' are ready to punish the crocodile who rises up to attack the sacred boat. The mouths of the dwellers in the waters are closed by Re, their throats blocked by Sekhmet, their tongues cut out by Thoth, their eyes blinded by Heka, the god of magic. The four gods who protect Re protect anyone who braves water, be they animal or human.

Here is another impressive spell: 'Come to me, master of the gods! Throw every sort of evil, every monster of the river onto land for me! Change them for me into pebbles on the mountain, like the fragments of pottery scattered by the side of the paths.'[18] A drastic solution, indeed: the harmful water creatures will not threaten anyone again once they have been transformed into pebbles.

To emerge victorious against the evil creatures dwelling in the waters, the magician does not hesitate to identify himself with Amun, Onuris, Montu or Soped in their role as warriors. Shocked, the underwater animals will not surface. They will drift in the current, their mouths sealed like the seven great boxes, closed for ever.[19]

Air

The *Coffin Texts* tell of an extraordinary feat of magic:[20] to become the four winds of the sky and know the name of the god who is responsible for the sky ladder that gives access to paradise. The magician has mastery over these four winds.[21] They give him the power to explore the entire universe. Thus, the south wind brings water, knowledge and life.

The magician's clothing is the life-giving breath. He has created the luminous sky to replace the darkness, he manifests himself in the storm clouds, the breadth of the sky is the measure of his stride.[22]

But the sky also contains dangers, in particular miasmas which causes illness. There are also spells to disperse the air tainted by the year.[23] The magician appeals to the vulture-goddess Nekhbet who holds the earth aloft. He asks her to come to him and wrap her great feathers tightly around him. Thus he will live in good health and receive the white crown, the insignia of power which is worn by the great magician of Heliopolis. He will sail on the cosmic ocean, in the barque of day, providing that he recites the spells correctly over a pair of vulture feathers.

The air one breathes must be purified by a magician. At certain times—in particular at the turn of the year—it carries dangerous elements (miasmas, negative fluids, illnesses). Only a purification by magic, which is, moreover, a part of a State ritual, can give humans invigorating air.

Fire

Harmful beings carry a flame, a destructive fire which is life-threatening. To quench it one must use water. But not just any water: it must be that of Nun, the primeval ocean in the guise of a cool wave.[24] The magician mingles the elements to wipe out the evil fire.*

The most frequent manifestation of the latter is a burn. Was not Horus himself burnt by the flame of Sekhmet, the lion-goddess[25] whose rage is dreadful? To treat any burn the magician must recall the legend of the infant Horus when a fire broke out. His mother was absent. The fire was too powerful for so small a child. None could save him. Coming from the weaving room where she was initiating some women into her mysteries, did not Isis extinguish the flame with her milk?

The spells must be recited over resin from the acacia tree, over a wheaten pancake, carob beans, bitter-apples and excrement, then all must be burned to make a substance to mix with the

---

* The eighth spell on the Behage plinth reveals the magician's method: 'Fire in the water, fire in the water, fire which came from the water! The flame of my mouth lit the fire, I extinguish it when it puts forth a flame. Water will quench the fire.'

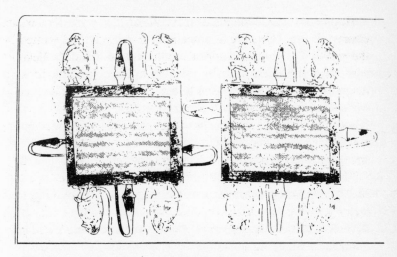

The baboons are grouped around a square basin containing the energy which is like fire. This is a representation of a truly 'central' power whose components may only be handled by specialists, and with the greatest possible care lest this perpetual fire becomes destructive.

milk of a woman who has given birth to a boy. Then the mixture is applied to the burn and the patient is bandaged with a leaf of the castor-oil plant.[26]

For a victim of a burn of scald, the magician must refer to Horus. The god was so badly injured that only Isis, the magician, was capable of inventing a remedy to avert the worst. There was no water near her. Thus the goddess was obliged to use a liquid from her own body: 'There is water in my mouth,' she said, 'and a Nile between my legs; I come to put out the fire.'[27]

The positive and creating fire is contained in the sun. The magician salutes it as it bursts from the shadows; it drives away the dark death that would snatch the child from its mother.[28] There are spells to disperse the clouds so that the sun can shine as usual.[29] Victory is never permanently won. The magic charm must be renewed daily. One piece of evidence for this is the papyrus leaf upon which is written the name of the dragon, then put in a box and thrown daily into the fire. When the sun rises the dragon's very being burns.[30]

A god's appearance is often accompanied by flames which

destroy any adversaries and harmful creatures. They are devoured by a divine fire. 'O rebels,' proclaims a spell, 'Amon's fire is against you, it will never be quenched. He who is hidden in his image, who is hidden in his form, curses you ... he hurls the fire against you to reduce you to ashes.'[31] Thus the most dangerous enemies see their plans reduced to nothing.*

The serpent uraeus on the pharaoh's brow is a living flame that burns the king's enemies to a cinder. The magician identifies himself with the uraeus. He becomes strong enough to cut off heads. The flame in his mouth is sharpened against the knives held by hostile gods, from whom he no longer has anything to fear.[33]

The destructive fire proves to be a protection as well. The *Coffin Texts* evoke the circle of fire that surrounds Re and protects him when he is in the cabin of the solar barque. The magician must make use of a spell to drive away the circle,[34] and for a moment the fire is quenched so that he may reach the interior of the sun.

'To enter into the solar disc' is a special theme with the initiates.[35] The magician has proved his competence by establishing a cosmic order to the glory of Re and opening the mysterious eye which gives light to humanity. An odd passage in the *Coffin Texts*[36] shows a divine being, seated on a throne and surrounded by ovals. This is the secret symbol of Re, enthroned in a serpent called Mehen. He evokes many cycles and years. Paths of fire protect this secret sun. The magician knows the dark ways by which Hu and Sha, the Word and Intuition, circulate. He knows 'the circuit of Re', the curve of the universe.

One spell serves for both entering the fire and leaving it.[37] The magician is a being whose shape is invisible in the midst of the fire. There he takes hold of a knife which is just a ray of light. The magician becomes the fire in the kingdom of the dead, in each part of the West,[38] a dark place to which he brings warmth.

---

* Another spell for the destruction of enemies by fire, which would also prevent the serpent from attacking: 'The flame against the sky, the arrow (of fire) against the earth! The arrow (of fire) against the earth, the flame against the sky.'[32]

*The barque of the sun with its divine crew. Day and night it sails through
the universe and guarantees the regulation of the creative energy wherever it
goes. If the barque stops, life ceases to circulate and the universe perishes.
That is why the astronomer-magician observes the heavens ceaselessly, so
that he may intervene if the barque encounters any difficulty.*

He becomes the flame that dies away before the wind, at the
ends of the earth and sky, which crosses the spaces.[39]

As master of fire, the magician lives in the harmony of the
spheres, Maat. He is also the master of eternity. He creates joy.
He knows the secret words written on the magic scrolls. He will
be as Re in the east of the sky, as Osiris in the world below.[40]

A spell is used 'to make the flame be born beneath the head
of the just', which refers to the famous hypocephalus, the disc
of cloth, papyrus or bronze placed beneath the mummy's head.[41]
This flame makes the body into a living being. It is the prototype
of the Christian halo, that aureole of fire which encircles the
heads of the saints. On this hypocephalus, often painted golden,
spells are written or protective spirits are painted.

The torches used during the rituals are prepared by those
initiated into the secrets of fire.[42] The magician is advised to
prepare four bowls made of clay mixed with incense, filled with
the milk of a white heifer, in which the flames are quenched at
the end of the ritual. He pronounces the words over four torches
of scarlet cloth impregnated with the oil of Libya. They are held
by four men on whose arms are drawn the name of the sons of
Horus. By respecting these rules, the initiate will have power
over the imperishable Stars.

6 The Magician in the Presence of the Gods

My hosts, the magicians of Luxor, were Moslems. But their Islamic faith showed itself to be receptive to the ancient divinities. The gods and goddesses of the time of the pharaohs have not entirely disappeared from the soil of Egypt. They are still present in the consciousness although under other names and other faces. Allah is the master of Arab magicians today . . . but a shadow lurks behind him. It is the shadow of an enigmatic god, sometimes an ibis, sometimes a baboon, a god who knows how to open the sealed papyri.

Thoth, Master of Magic

Thoth, the lord of Hermopolis, is the master of hieroglyphs and magic. In his town a great temple was built whose secret crypts housed magical papyri written by the hand of the god. The magician likens himself to Thoth, taking the same animal shape: 'I am he who is in the nest, like the venerable ibis, Thoth is my name.'[1]

Thoth, the magician, is the model for all his disciples. The guardian of wisdom, inventor of the sacred language, astronomer, mathematician, he healed the Eye of Horus, the measure of all things. According to the *Stela of Metternich*, Thoth is invoked as the god 'equipped' with magical power. He can exorcise the effects of a poison, so that the patient is not harmed beyond help. He repels the rebels who rise against Re without cease. He comes from the sky, on the order of the sun-god, to protect the weak by day or night.[2]

The magician appeals to Re to obtain Thoth's help. 'O old man who becomes young again in his own time, old man who becomes a child again, may you make Thoth come at my call.'[3] Thoth comes down from the sky. He fights the scorpion's poison, he heals those who are stung, particularly Horus, the son of Isis.[4] He says to the suffering god, 'Your head is yours (and it also wears the crowns), your eyes are yours, your nose is yours, your arms and forearms are yours, your heart is yours, your hands are yours, your belly is yours, your phallus is yours, your thighs are yours, your feet are yours'; as a result of this bodily integrity: 'You are the head of the land of the south, the north, the west and the east. You see like Re.' Thanks to Thoth, the gods possess a healthy mind in a healthy body and initiates enjoy the same privilege. The magician is a healing god: 'I am Thoth,' he states, 'the elder son of Re, whom Atum and the Ennead sent so that Horus would regain his health for the sake of his mother Isis, as one who was stung was healed.'[5]

But Thoth is also a magician who punishes. He is required to sharpen his knife which cuts out the hearts of those who would oppose the king when he comes to Osiris.[6] As a formidable power, Thoth intervenes effectively by dispelling natural disturbances and watching over the equilibrium of the universe. Thus it is Thoth, the dog-headed ape of seven cubits in stature, who prevents an inundation from being too great.[7]

The master of magicians is not miserly with his knowledge. He teaches scribes, those who seek, and seers, making them skilful in their art. A *Book of Hours* sets out Thoth's extensive duties: 'Lord of writing, pre-eminent in the House of Books, powerful in magic, who possesses the sacred eye . . . heart of Re, tongue of Atum, guide of the gods who measure out everything, who count out time, the chief justice and vizier, the messenger of Re, who exorcises demons, who puts all things in their proper place, Thoth who completes the Eye of Re and the Eye of Horus.'[8]

These documents indicate that Thoth rules intelligence and intellectual activity in general. To him are attributed writing, the words of the gods, the separation of the languages that give each race its own identity, laws, the basis of society, history, the official royal documents, the rituals and the calendar. How could he fail, after that, being a god and a magician as well, to accomplish all this?

The scribes and magicians do not always behave well. One passage of the *Pyramid Texts* recounts a strange episode:[9] 'Scribe, scribe, break your palette in pieces, break your brushes, destroy your scrolls! O Re, put pressure on the magician, chase him from his position and put me in his place ... for I am he!' The same collection[10] offers an explanation: the king must not be deprived of the magic which is his to hold. Evil scribes who would like to keep these powers for themselves will see the tools of their trade broken. The good magician must often struggle with colleagues who would deflect magic from its original goal, the protection of the royal person.

A useful step is to become Thoth's secretary. The holder of this office will see the opening of the god's chest after the seals are broken. The magician also makes himself acquainted with the most secret documents, those known as the 'funerary texts'[11] which hold the keys to survival. Admitted into the circle of the gods, the magician introduces himself as one of them. Seth is at his right hand, Horus on his left. The magician does not come empty-handed for he brings the amulets which are Horus' protection.

Thoth steps in to advance the initiate along the path of knowledge. It is he who brings him into the solar disc so that he may gain true power.[12] Thoth enobles the just man whose head is set firmly upon his shoulders. He receives a sceptre in the barque of the night into which he is admitted by the sun's followers. The paths of the Master of all are revealed to him.[13]

But Thoth does not offer his secret to all and sundry. One must show oneself to be worthy, to seek and find the secrets. Such a discovery is attested to in several Egyptian texts. Chapter 30B of the *Book of the Dead* is a spell which prevents a man's heart opposing him in the Netherworld. It must be recited over a scarab of jade, mounted in electrum with a silver ring which is put about the neck of the dead man. This text is of considerable importance since his knowledge of it will protect the initiate from condemnation when he appears before the tribunal beyond the grave. Now, the spell was discovered beneath the feet of a statue of Thoth, which dates from the time of Mycerinos. There was also a belief that the text was carved on a faience brick in the image of the foundation stone upon which the temple rests. Each magician must seek and discover the spell which was left by Thoth as a legacy to his pupils.

As one can see from all this, Thoth is the patron of Egyptian magicians, to whom they owe the revelation of their science. This is why the accomplished magician introduces himself as Thoth descended from the sky (the *Metternich Stela*). When he recites the ritual, he quite legitimately declares: 'I am Thoth, master of the divine words, he who acts as interpreter to all the gods.'[14]

From Horus to Bes

The magician gods are thought of as 'pantheons'—that is, as a power 'accompanied by its separate powers broken down into a visible form, analysed and juxtaposed in some way, in the image of the god who contains them.'[15]

Moreover, the magician god holds the insignia of his power, such as the sceptres, and wears the crowns. These complex divinities, prized in late papyri, passed down into the talismen of the Middle Ages in the West, thus prolonging the influence of Egyptian magic.

In the beginning, the magician, in his role as Horus, received the protection of heaven and earth, against the dead, male and female, in the south, north east or west.[16] Indeed, Horus' words give exceptional protection. They drive off death, make the breathless breathe again, renew life, lengthen the years, extinguish fire, heal the victim of poison, unless the man is fated to die. The magic of Horus will deflect arrows from their target, and pacify anger in the heart of a wrathful man.[17] Thoth, the master of magicians, glorifies Horus on land and water. He salutes him, who was borne by the divine cow, whom Isis brought into the world. He spoke his name, recited his magic, wrought wonders with his incantations, used the power that came from his mouth.[18]

Horus is invoked as the supreme son and heir, bull child of the bull and cow of the sky, whose powerful utterances, the mighty words passed on by his father the Earth and his mother the Sky, enable him to immobilise the reptiles in the sky, earth and water, the lions of the desert, the crocodiles in the river. These harmful creatures will be reduced to the condition of the stones of the desert or pieces of broken vases.[19]

When Isis comes to Horus she teaches him that he is her son in the region of heaven. The offspring of the primeval Ocean, he shows himself in the form of a great heron born on the top of a willow tree at Heliopolis, the brother of a prophetic fish which tells of things to come. A cat fed him in the house of Neith, the patroness of weaving. A sow and a dwarf protected him.[20] Clearly, all is magic in this divine education.

Every part of Horus' body is given life by magic so that he may be totally possessed by the forces from above and carry out their tasks—fight his father's enemies, vanquish Seth the rebel, and reign over the four cardinal points. The protector of royalty, Horus' main role is that of healing god. He is seen trampling upon crocodiles, holding scorpions and dangerous insects in his hand, proving that he has nothing to fear from creatures that bring death. The other fundamental role of Horus is that of shepherd. Horus the herdsman guards his flock. But it was threatened by savage beasts. Isis and Nephthys, who fashion amulets, intervened. Thus were the mouths of lions and hyenas closed. By magic, Horus hunts them, robs them of their strength and strikes them blind. In his identity of shepherd-god the magician makes the wild beasts scatter to the four winds.[21] The sky opens, releasing favourable influences for the peasant who in complete safety takes pleasure in all his property. No evil being will come near the field.*

---

* On the subject of 'agricultural' magic, we should point out that the magician also becomes the barley of Lower Egypt, the bush of life which comes from Osiris, growing on his ribs to nourish men, making the gods divine and spiritualising the spirits. The initiate is the 'dried grain' of the living, the food of those who follow him on earth.[22]

In the 18th Dynasty there arose the curious figure of Shed the Saviour who gives protection against animals and dangerous insects. Shed is a young man who kills dangerous beasts with his arrows, or seizes them by the tail. At a later date he is confused with Horus the child. He is represented on steĺae standing on two crocodiles, a mask of Bes over his head, surrounded by magic spells. These monuments, sometimes modest, sometimes of considerable size, are true talismen, which guarantee the State's safety.[23]

Another 'magic' god is Shu, who created himself and whose shape is invisible. He is filled with creative power, calms the sky, and orders the Two Lands.[24] Now, the magician is Shu, son of Atum. He was created in his nose and came forth from his nostrils. The magician knows the science of the infinite spaces; to prove it, he recites a spell over the eight gods who uphold the universe, a spell which has been drawn with yellow paint and ochre of Nubia upon a man's hand.[25]

In the Late Dynastic Period, the fame of Shu, son of Re, grew. He was thought to support the sky. Standing in his chariot he drives off the wild beasts. He is seen as the 'Saviour', as a magical power capable of snatching man from the grasp of evil.

The god Seth is known as the assassin of Osiris. But he fulfils a more positive role. When Horus, suffering from a headache, lies on a cushion, his brother Seth watches over him, and prevents him being attacked by demons who wish to paralyse him.

This divine act is repeated on earth. The magician acts like a weaver. He cuts off a piece of material, ties seven knots in it and attaches it to the patient's big toe.[26] To succeed in this, the magus must take the identity of Seth, who has considerable power:[27] 'I am he who has divided that which was reunited,' he declares, 'I am he who is full of vigour and great in power, Seth.'

Let us not forget that the dead man has been given a perfect shroud, which is also that of the initiate being reborn to life as a spirit—Seth's skin.[28] The house of resurrection will then be the very being of the 'enemy', the adversary who has been vanquished and mastered by magic power. All the techniques of the martial arts rest on the same principle: to use the strength of the opponent who seeks to destroy you to increase your own power.

Seth is an efficient healer. In a special spell against the mysterious 'Asian illness' an appeal is made to Seth who calms the sea. Thus the bodily fluids themselves will also be at peace and the illness will go away. If necessary, the sick man will be confined and his mouth closed with the skin of a tortoise.[29]

A magical papyrus from Paris teaches us that the magician invokes the gods with the aid of a vase. He speaks to Seth-Typhon, who is thought of as the god of gods. The magician is so bold because Seth's power enables him to make the gods come at his bidding.[30]

Bes was the most popular magician god in late Egypt. He existed in pharaonic Egypt where he played the role of the bringer of joy, who conquered by means of victory over the powers of darkness. Bes is a bearded dwarf, with a lion's face and twisted

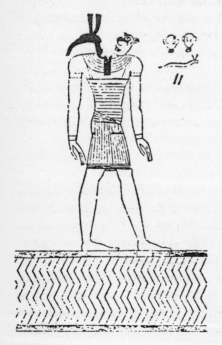

A drawing of the god who is called 'Two-faced', i.e. those of Seth and Horus, brothers who are at the same time both enemies and inseparable, united in the same being. This double Person, formed from two symbolic entities who fight unceasingly to keep their supremacy over the universe, is in reality One: for all is in the perception of the magician who knows how to discern unity in duality.

legs. He sticks his tongue out—a symbol of the transmission of the Word which can often be seen later portrayed on columns in cathedrals. Bes appears on stelae, vases, amulets and temple walls. He terrifies anyone who does not know him, and scares away the incompetent magician. With his knife he attacks demons and puts them to flight. His body is often spangled with eyes which serve as protection against the evil eye. That is why he is much concerned with human daily life, giving special protection to women in labour.

Bes is also in charge of the eastern frontier of the Delta, for it is from there that invaders come. There also, each morning, the sun battles victoriously against Apophis the dragon.

At Abydos, in his role as the host of the temple of Seti I, Bes pronounces oracles and heals the sick.[31] The *Brooklyn Magical Papyrus*[32] tells that Seth of the seven faces banishes the dead, enemies and adversaries both male and female, and the sow who devours the West. Bes marshals the considerable forces of Amon-Re who is the head of Karnak, the ram with the wonderful breast, the great lion born of himself, the great god of the beginning of time, lord of the sky and the earth, he whose name is hidden, the giant a million cubits in height.

Being very popular, Bes for a long time resisted Christianity which demoted him to the status of an evil genie. But every Egyptian knows that the bearded, laughing god is always present, hidden in the temples. There are many who still seek his favours.

The Goddesses of Magic

The idea of magic is immediately associated with the name of Isis, she who knew the secret name of the supreme god. Isis has at her disposal the magic which Geb, the earth god, gave her to protect her son Horus. She can close up the mouth of every snake, ward off every desert lion, every river crocodile and each biting reptile, from her child. With a word she turns away the effect of poison and makes it turn back its destructive fire, and gives breath to those who lack it. The malign humours which disturb the human body obey Isis. The 'vessels', at her words, purge themselves of any evil they contain.[33] Anyone who is stung, bitten or attacked appeals to Isis of the artful mouth, identifying themselves with Horus who appeals to his mother for help. She will come, make magical gestures and show herself reassuringly while soothing her son. Nothing serious can harm the child of the great goddess. One who rises, like Horus, from the sky and the primeval waters cannot die.[34] Is not Isis the Mother from whom all comes and to whom all returns?

Nut, the sky goddess, reigns over a magic cosmos. Often, the symbol of Nut, a winged woman or a female vulture, is seen on the breasts of mummies. There is a spell, used by the goddess herself, to define her action: 'I am your mother Nut, I spread myself above you in my name of the sky. Having entered my mouth, you go out between my thighs, like the Sun each day.'[35]

Mut, whose name means 'mother', appears among the composite magical figures. The words of power are spoken over a figure of the goddess Mut with three heads (woman, lion, vulture[36]). A winged goddess, equipped with a phallus, and with a lion's claws, Mut, drawn upon a band of red material, gives the magician the power not to be repulsed in the kingdom of the dead, and to receive a star from the sky as a gift.

The Seven Hathors are Egyptian fairies. Wearing a serpent uraeus on their foreheads, they hold each other by the hand forming a chain of union. The goddess Hathor herself leads her seven daughters. In fact she takes the form of seven kindly divinities who grant a favourable destiny to the new-born. They delight the world with music and dancing. Their role is to guide and give predictions, not to fix destinies immovably. But the utterance of a prediction, because of the magic of the Word, often becomes the reality. A stela kept at La Haye dating from the 19th Dynasty shows the Seven Hathors who promise descendants to a priest of Thoth in exchange for the service which he renders them. Between the sorceresses and the skilled devotees of the god of magic, contact was easy.

Daughters of the Light, the Seven Hathors hold bandages of red yarn with which they create knots. According to the number of knots, seven being quite the most beneficial sign, the destiny of the person with whom the fairies are concerned is confirmed or denied.

The lion-beaded goddess Sekhmet is formidable. She rules bands of messenger genies, armed with knives, who wander through the earth, bringing illness, famine and death, notably during those sensitive times of the year, the periods of transition when evil is swallowed up—the passage from one year to another, the end of a decade, the end of the month or even the end of day and beginning of night.[37] These terrifying hordes are exorcised by the most competent magicians firstly at State level and then in the private sphere. To pacify Sekhmet's anger, one must use an amulet or statuette representing the goddess. Evil influence then becomes beneficent, power is cleansed of its impurities. On the last day of the year the lion-goddess is invoked while recalling the role of the assassins who came from the Evil Eye sowing panic and darkness, hurling their darts from their mouths: may they stay far from the magician! They will have no power over him, for he is Re, he is Sekhmet herself! These words must be spoken over a piece of fine linen upon which the gods are drawn. The magician offers them bread and beer, burns incense, makes twelve knots and put the material on the neck of the one who wished to be protected. To ward off the murderers and arsonists of Sekhmet, the magician takes the identity of Horus, the unique. He speaks the spells over a wooden cane, holding it in his hand. Then he must leave his house and walk round it.[38]

In the reign of Amenophis III many beautiful statues of the goddess Sekhmet were sculpted. She is called 'she whose power is as great as infinity'. The epithets found on the statues form a gigantic litany, evoking a Sekhmet-flame which repels the dragon and fights Pharaoh's enemies. Such a force is difficult to handle for it can destroy the world. But it is thanks to it that Pharaoh maintains his vitality. He is living among the living on condition that Sekhmet is appeased and controlled. That is why the statues of Sekhmet protect the entrances to the sacred places, denying access to the impure and unfit.

The ritual year is personified by the serpent uraeus which, to symbolise the multiplicity of days, becomes 365 serpents set

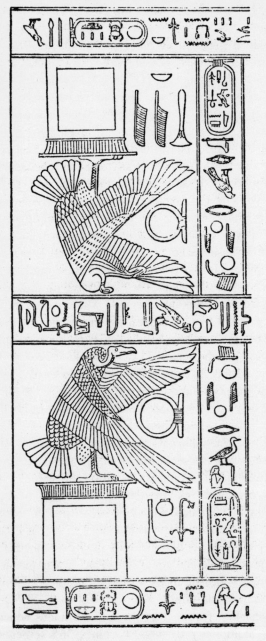

The two goddesses who protect royalty: Nekhbet, a vulture, and Wadjet, a winged cobra. Between their wings, the hieroglyph Chen, which evokes the movement of life, truly a 'ring of power' which presents the circle of the universe. This is portrayed as a knotted and plaited cord, the perfect symbol of coherence.

around the royal crown. Now there were 365 statues of Sekhmet
(or two series of 365): each day it was necessary to gain the
favours of the goddess so that she would give out a positive force
and protect the pharaoh, the temple and even the homes of private
individuals.[39]

Dwarfs and Giants

There is a spell in which a 'good dwarf' plays an important part
with the placenta which is asked to 'descend' so that the birth
will go well and the mother be happily delivered. The goddess
Hathor herself places her hand upon the labouring woman. Magic
spells are pronounced four times over a clay dwarf, placed on
the head of the woman who is in painful labour.[40]

An appeal is made to the heavenly dwarf who has a large
head, long hindquarters and short thighs: may he take care of
the magician by night and day, although his rather unpleasing
appearance is that of an old ape.[41]

Often the god of magic has the shape of a dwarf. The *Brooklyn
Magical Papyrus* offers some particularly interesting vignettes.
We see a man with a head of Bes, standing holding a sceptre
and *ankh*-sign in two of his hands. But he is provided with many
arms holding knives, lances and snakes. His body is covered with
eyes. He is winged.[42] Above the head of Bes there are many
animal heads—cat, ape, lion, bull, hippopotamus, crocodile and
falcon, all of them surmounted by the Ram's horns from which
emerge six knives and six serpents. Beneath the feet of the god
is a serpent swallowing his own tail and encircling some animals.
The strange figure is placed in a circle of flames.[43]

To these fascinating apparitions the magician can add that of
a giant whom he can cause to intervene so that the order of the
world will be respected. Serge Sauneron connected this symbol
with the idea of the immensity of god who upholds the sky and
whose stride can cover the entire universe: whence the notion of
a being who measures a million cubits, a good giant of magic.[44]

7 The Magician's Battles

The procession of gods and goddesses, the magic litany with its strange echoes, the world forgotten and yet so near . . . my hosts in Luxor still knew the secrets of the magical divinities of ancient Egypt. Yet theirs was not a blind devotion. 'Magic,' confided the Old Man, 'is a battle. The gods must yield to your thought. The goddesses must fall in love with you. Otherwise, they would be your implacable enemies.' 'Must it always be a struggle?' I asked. 'In magic, always,' he replied.

Tales and Legends

The tales of ancient Egypt, which are literary works of exceptional merit as much for their content as for their style, show the magicians at work. One of them, which is set in the Old Kingdom,[1] tells the story of a deceived husband. However this unfortunate spouse was not just an ordinary man, but a lector-priest and a highly qualified magician. He made a wax crocodile, seven thumbs length long, and uttered a spell: 'Whoever shall come to bathe in my pool, lay hold of him.' By the Word, the waxen crocodile was given a magic soul which would make him real if the need arose. The magician asked his servant to put the crocodile in the water when his wife's lover came to bathe.

The time came. The magician's wife and her lover met in the paradisiacal garden of this high official. The lover decided to bathe in this enchanting pool. The servant, obeying his master, put the crocodile into the water and it was transformed into a very real reptile seven cubits long, and held the man at the bottom of the pool for seven years.

When the magician returned home, accompanied by Pharaoh who honoured him with his friendship, he wished to show the Lord of Egypt a great wonder. He ordered the crocodile to bring his wife's lover back to the surface. The monster was so enormous that he rather frightened Pharaoh. The lector-priest easily seized the reptile which immediately became a wax crocodile again. Then the magician told the king of his misfortune. Pharaoh pronounced judgement: the crocodile should take what was his. The monster seized the condemned man, sank to the bottom of the pool and no one ever knew where he went with his prey. As for the adulterous wife, she was burnt and her ashes thrown into the Nile.

Another tale, from the reign of Cheops, tells of a magician's battle not against a rival in love but with pharaoh in person. There was at that time a wonderful magician called Djedi, one hundred and ten years old, who still ate five hundred loaves and a side of beef and drank a hundred pitchers of beer. Cheops needed to know how many secret rooms there were in the temple of Thoth. Now Djedi knew this. He was therefore fetched from his home and brought to court, into the presence of the king of Egypt. 'Is it true what they say,' said Cheops, 'that you know how to put back in place a head that has been cut off?' 'Yes,' said the magician. Pharaoh wished to verify this. He ordered that a prisoner be executed and his body brought.

This was the moment for the magician to do battle. 'No,' he said gravely, 'not a human being, my sovereign lord, for it is forbidden for the holy followers of God to do such a thing.' A critical moment, and the tension was palpable. Pharaoh, a magician himself, accepted the warning. A goose was brought, then an ox. Their heads were cut off and the magician put them back again. He thus saved their lives, even in the most difficult circumstances. Later he revealed to the pharaoh the means by which he might know the number of secret rooms in the temple of Thoth, the master of magic.

*   *   *

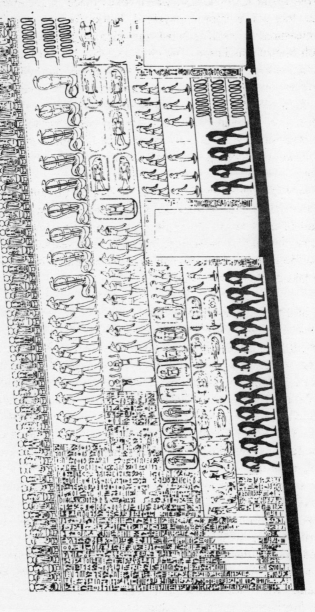

The regions of the other world: long lines of genies, serpents, powers contained within protective cartouches, people without heads and with their hands tied behind their backs symbolising the dark forces. All are moving towards the same goal, transmutation by the Light.

The *Tale of the Oarswomen*, which takes place in the time of Snefru, tells of a more 'physical' battle for the magician who measured himself against the element of Water. The pharaoh Snefru was bored. The chief lector-priest, the magician Djadjaemankh, advised him to go for a sail in his ship with some beautiful women. The leader of the oarswomen, who was seated at the stern of the boat, let fall a turquoise necklet in the form of a fish into the water. Immediately she ceased rowing. The whole crew stopped. Pharaoh was prepared to replace the jewellery, but the beauty was stubborn: she wanted that pendant and no other.

Snefru appealed to the magician. He uttered the spell which must be used to gain mastery of water. Then he calmly placed one half of the lake on top of the other, and found the pendant which he returned to its owner. Then, so as to leave things the way he found them, the magician carefully restored the first half of the lake to its normal place.

A tale of the time of Rameses II tells the story of a magical battle against the illness of a young princess who was marked for the highest destiny. This young woman, the princess of the land of Bakhtan, was to marry the great Rameses who had fallen in love with her. But illness seized her. Pharaoh appealed to the most learned men but they could not heal her. Since human magicians had failed, the magic power embodied in the statue of the god Khonsu had to be sought. On being consulted, it nodded in approval at what was proposed: it was carried, with due reverence, to the land of the princess. The voyage lasted seventeen months. The divine statue worked its magic on the young woman and she was cured. The demon who had made her ill spoke with the Egyptian god, swearing that he would henceforth be his slave. The prince of Bakhtan, amazed by the magical powers of Egypt, decided to keep this wonderful statue. But after three years and nine months he saw, in a dream, the divine power escaping from the statue in the form of a golden hawk and taking wing for Egypt. Frightened, he let the statue go.

*   *   *

The tale of Satni Khamois is one of the jewels of world literature. Satni Khamois, the king's son, studied the books in the sacred script, particularly those of the House of Life, and stelae, and knew the properties of amulets and talismen. He also wrote. Of him it was said, 'This is a magician without equal in the land of Egypt.'

One day an old man played a trick on him. He knew of a book written in Thoth's own hand and could lead him to its hiding-place. There were two spells written in it. 'If you use the first,' said the old man, 'you will charm the sky, the earth, hell, the mountains and the waters; you will know the birds of the air and the reptiles of every kind; you will see the fish, for the divine face will make them rise to the surface. If you read the second spell, when you are in the tomb you will have the same form as you have on earth: you will see the sun rise in the sky, its train of gods, the moon in the form it had when it first appeared.'

· This wonderful book was hidden in a necropolis, in the tomb of a king's son. Satni went down into it. He found it as bright as if the sunlight reached it, for light shone from the book. The name of the king's son was Neferkaptah. The souls of his wife and son were also there.

These souls talked with Satni, and tried to dissuade him from taking the book which was the source of many ills. Neferkaptah, in fact, had learnt where the book was—in the middle of a river and in an iron box. In the iron box was a bronze box, in the bronze box, a palm-wood box, in the palm-wood box, a box of ivory and ebony, in the box of ivory and ebony, a silver box, in the silver box, a golden box, and in this one the book lay. All around was a seething nest of snakes, scorpions and all manner of reptiles. The final barrier was an immortal serpent which was coiled around the final box.

Neferkaptah killed the immortal serpent twice, and twice it came back to life. He fought the reptile a third time, cut it in two pieces and scattered sand over them so that the serpent could not regain its former shape. Then he threw away the book with all its enchantments.

But he had gone too far. The god Thoth was troubled. He

complained to Re. The sun god laid a spell on the magician and overwhelmed him with all kinds of misfortunes, chiefly by drowning his wife and child. Before he himself could drown, the magician clasped the book to his chest.

Satni would not listen to any counsel of prudence. He gambled for the book in a game of chess with Neferkaptah, lost the game but nevertheless kept possession of the book of spells. Bewitched by a woman with whom he had fallen in love, he had his own children killed so that he could sleep with her. These terrible enchantments were Neferkaptah's vengeance.

Satni awoke from his nightmare. It was only a bad dream. His children still lived. Guided by Neferkaptah's spirit, he left the remains of his wife and son to rest in peace and did not touch the cursed book.

The tale of Siusire, son of Setna, tells of another magical contest which this time did not end in failure. This text is written in demotic on the back of some Greek papyri in the British Museum.[2]

Setna was distressed. His wife could not comfort him. His son came. Why was his father so low, so sad? What was troubling him? 'You are too young, you would not understand.' The son insisted. The father explained. An Ethiopian official had come to Egypt, carrying a sealed letter. He had laid down a challenge. Could anyone read it without opening it? None of the Egyptian wise men could do it. Egypt was humiliated by the land of the Negroes. That was why Setna was ill.

His son Siusire laughed. 'Rise, father,' said Siusire, 'I know how to read the letter without breaking the seal.' His father did not believe him. He put him to the test with some books which were in his cellar. His son passed the test. Siusire therefore played a part in the drama which unfolded at the court of Egypt.

The Ethiopian magician decided to plunge the land of the pharaohs into darkness. Using wax he made a litter with four porters and brought them to life by magic. He ordered them to take the king of Egypt to the king of Ethiopia, which they did!

Pharaoh was given five hundred strokes of the cane and then returned to Egypt. Alerted, the court magician used his knowledge to prevent the worst—a repeat of this humiliation. He called on Thoth, the inventor of magic who built the earth and the sky: let him save pharaoh from the Ethiopian magic.

Thoth appeared in a dream to this magician (who was called Hor, son of Panesi). He advised him to go to the library of the temple of Khnum where he would find a scroll of papyri written in his own hand. He should take a copy and return it to its proper place. With the help of this document, Hor made protective amulets. With their help, pharaoh was not dragged off to Ethiopia against his will. Horus, in his turn, made a litter with four porters in wax and brought it to life. They brought the king of Ethiopia to Egypt where he received five hundred strokes of the cane. When he awoke, he was bruised and concluded that he had fallen under an evil spell.

Twice more the king of Ethiopia was thus ill-treated. The negro magician decided to go to Egypt to confront his rival. The contest between the magicians could now really take place. Horus the Egyptian made the rain fall and extinguished a fire. The Ethiopian made the clouds gather over the court of Egypt so that no one could recognise anyone else. With a magic spell, Horus wiped the sky clean. His adversary created a great stone arch to separate Egypt from its pharaoh, and the pharaoh from the sky. Horus created a ship, placed the arch in it and thus bore it into the sky. Sensing that he was on the brink of defeat, the Ethiopian made himself invisible so that he could flee. But Horus made him reappear in the shape of a bird of prey fallen on its back. A bird catcher captured it to stab it. The mother of the Ethiopian magician, sensing that her son was in danger of death, came to Egypt in the form of a goose. Horus recognised her and made her submit. She became a negress again and implored him to have mercy on her son and herself. They swore that they would not return to Egypt for 1,500 years.

Now, this Horus had returned from the West, 1,500 years after his death, to battle with the enemy magician and save the honour of Egypt. Osiris had let him come back to earth to accomplish this mission in the form of ... Siusire who, like a shadow, disappeared before the eyes of the pharaoh and his father.

The sceptic Lucien, in the *Sacred Scribe of Memphis*, relates the story of a celebrated magical combat which is the origin of the legend of the sorcerer's apprentice, too inexperienced for the forces which he was trying to master. The storyteller was staying in Egypt to study. He went to see the statue of Memnon and hear the strange sound it gives at the rising of the sun. Miraculously Memnon gave out an oracle in seven verses. On going back up the Nile, the storyteller met a scribe from Memphis who had spent twenty-three years in the crypts where Isis had taught him magic. He knew how to ride on crocodiles and control monsters. The traveller gained his confidence. On their arrival at a hostelry, the magician took the bar from the door, or a broom or perhaps a pestle, covered it with clothes, said a spell which brought it to life and made it walk. Everyone thought it was a man. The animated object fulfilled all the two travellers' desires—it brought water and provisions. Then it became a broom or a pestle again. But the magician would not reveal his secret. One day, his over-inquisitive companion hid and heard the spell—a three-syllable word. He tried to imitate the master, clothed a pestle, pronounced the spell and commanded it to bring water. Total success. But how was it to be stopped? The animated pestle kept on bringing water and flooded the house. The apprentice sorcerer, frightened, cut the pestle in two—with disastrous consequences for there were now two water carriers. Happily, when the magician returned, he restored order but disappeared for ever with his secret.

The Battle Against the Enemy

The magician's enemy is the rebel, who rises against the order of the world, provoking the gods to anger, and, crying with a loud voice, summons into action the forces of evil.[3]

According to the inscriptions on the statue of Djed-her,[4] dramatic events occur. A voice is raised in the temple. There is lamentation in the palace. A crime has been committed. The gods weep. Re, who has not heard, appears at last and repulses the Enemy who was trying to destroy harmony.

The magician knows that this Enemy, who is a focus of negativity, is present in this world as in the other, and seeks to put an end to life by every means. A man who suffers sickness has the Enemy within him and only the magic art can drive him from his body. The *Bremner-Rhind Papyrus* states that the magician is inspired by the Creator to conquer the rebel who, with dreadful intent, rises up against the sun each day to prevent it being reborn.

The battle of the sun against the demon of darkness repeats itself eternally. The sick man—or the patient—accompanies the sun-god on his voyage. The most dramatic moment is the rising of the sun in the east when the sun is red and Re bathes in the blood of the wounds received in battle.[5] The struggle takes place on the Isle of Flame, the special world where the light confronts the living forces in darkness, where magical power overcomes chaos. In the 'Houses of Life' this 'Island of the Flame' was the place where the trainee underwent testing before receiving the secret of magic from his Brothers. The Elder who passed on this wisdom was compared to the Creator. At the end of his initiation and at each important act, the magician paid homage to the One who created himself, who shows himself by the Light of the East, whose nature is hidden, the old man who is young and exists in all things.

The magician appeals to the great god to come down from the heights of the sky and destroy the enemies. He also asks help from the Ennead, the confraternity of Nine Creators, in overthrowing the evil which threatens Horus and makes the heart fail. The magician has the necessary scientific skill to re-establish the proper circulation of energy both for men and gods.

The magician challenges the enemy, whether male or female. He proclaims his power, he inspires fear in spirits. He is feared, for he claims to be a god who commands evil forces to submit and be gone. He proves that he is stronger than they. He questions them, often very harshly, going so far as to threaten them. If the enemy suspected the slightest weakness, the battle would be lost to the magician and human life threatened at its very roots. Politeness, which mostly shows itself in a refined civilisation, often obliges the magician to apologise to his supernatural enemy, but he can do no other, for he is possessed by a power which is superior to evil.

Here is an example of the way in which a magician addresses his enemies:[6] 'If they raised their hands against him, it would be like raising their hands against the man a million cubits tall who stands on the thirty peaks of the land of Kush (the Sudan), the god with bloodshot eyes who hates coitus; he has an animal head . . .' Even a demon, we must admit, would be terrified by such an apparition.*

There is a special book of magic for repelling enemies. It is contained in a box of acacia wood. When the good spell is uttered it is the magic power itself that speaks. It reveals the mysteries of Osiris and the nature of the gods. The magician initiated into the secrets of this book has unusual mastery of the divine forces. He can even make Osiris serve him and recognise him as an expert in the supernatural. He threatens the god that if he shows defiance, he will hinder the sacred sailings to the holy town of Busiris and Abydos, destroy his *ba* and his body, and set fire to his tomb.[7]

The enemy willingly embodies himself in the form of a monster named Apophis, a sort of serpent dragon who is the ultimate rebel. There is, moreover, a 'Book for the repulsing of Apophis'. The magician asks the gods to intervene to prevent the dragon developing normally, and that his name should be destroyed, both his soul and spirit, his shadow, his bones, his hair, that he should not have children and heirs, that his seed and his egg should atrophy, that his magical power be smothered and that he should find a place neither in the sky nor the earth.[8]

The practitioner utters the following incantation over a small wax figure of Apophis:[9] 'Your poison will not enter my limbs,

---

* These remarks are not reserved solely for the magician; they also apply to the 'patients' whom he wishes to protect. That is why the spell specifies: 'To pronounce these words over an image which is drawn, once when it is copied onto a new leaf of papyrus, and again when it is put on the man's neck.'

for my limbs are those of Atum . . . your numbness will not enter my limbs, my safeguard is all the gods, eternally.' Spell VI of the *Behaque Plinth* helps in driving away Apophis, the demon of darkness, 'the fallen, the rebel, thought of as Re's intestine, the being who has neither arms nor legs'. The monster's head has been cut off.

The *Stela of Metternich* nevertheless states that the dragon Apophis is useful to Re because his flame can feed the rays of the sun. In fact Apophis is not killed; he is controlled.

With the word, the magician neutralises the cursed dragon: 'Vanish Apophis, enemy of Re! (to be said four times). Tremble, go far away from the one who is in the naos, be annihilated, rebel! Fall on your face, may your face be blinded!' When the dragon's paths are blocked, he has no more power, his heart fails. He is wounded by the knives that are thrust into his body. His head is cut off and thrown in the fire.[10] To conquer Apophis, one must first glorify the power of Light, the joy it inspires. Then one spits on the dragon: Re burns him with his flames so that the barque continues to sail in the skies in total safety, until the monster reappears.

The struggle with Apophis is a fight against all the enemies of the light, who are also ordered to fall on their faces. The magician will make them perish, will tear them to pieces. They will no longer have a name. It is the flame of the Eye of Horus that will exterminate them; it is Sekhmet, the deified fire, who will destroy them. Thus will Apophis and his allies, the tortoise, the oryx, the children of rebels, the adversaries of the gods and of pharaoh be beaten.

To be sure of being totally effective the names of one's enemies, with those of their fathers, mothers and children, are written in green on a leaf of papyrus and carved on wax figurines. One spits on them, grinds them beneath one's feet, pierces them through, burns them in the grate at precise times of the day or night, on particular days of the month. Magic and astronomy are closely mingled. Moreover the victory over Apophis takes place in a cosmic setting; it is Re himself who strikes the decisive blow, in the presence of the gods of the south, north, east and west. Orion chains the dragon in the southern sky, the Great Bear fetters him in the northern sky.

Apophis is not the only hateful being who must be fought. There are innumerable spells against equally terrifying individuals, such as a certain Shakek, a demon from the sky and the earth, who has his tongue in his anus, eats 'the bread of his backside' (his excrement) and attacks the initiates. 'Behind, turn round!' the magician who manages to shut his mouth and cut off his tongue, commands. The monster will be cut into pieces. His name will be suppressed, providing that the magic words are uttered over an arrow of wax.[11]

To be certain of his powers the magician makes a pilgrimage to the holy towns of Pe and Dep in the Delta, and he returns from there identified with a knife. That is why he says his limbs are made of iron.[12] Possessing that special weapon, being himself that weapon, the magician is able to employ his power against every enemy who might oppose him.

Other instruments that will discourage the adversary are the magic ivories, knives or sticks upon which are portrayed creatures which may be either friends or opponents of the sun in his struggles against the shadows. The magician who uses them is an 'illuminated one' who, like the Light, conquers those who disturb the cosmic order. Inscriptions and images bring to life these protective objects which are often used to protect children from all peril. Named with his own name, identified with the sun, the child who has been protected by magic relives the passion and dramas of the gods and also their victories.[13]

A favourite manifestation of the malevolent powers is the evil eye, which is particularly dreadful. There is a way of combating its influence—to use the arrow of Sekhmet and the magic of Thoth. It is also essential to ask for the aid of Isis and Nephthys, and to trust in the lance of Horus which will fix itself right inside the enemy's head. The adversary will finish his sad existence in the furnace of a magician of the House of Life who will blind those who might cast the evil eye upon a just man.[14]

The magician, to preserve his integrity, launches an attack

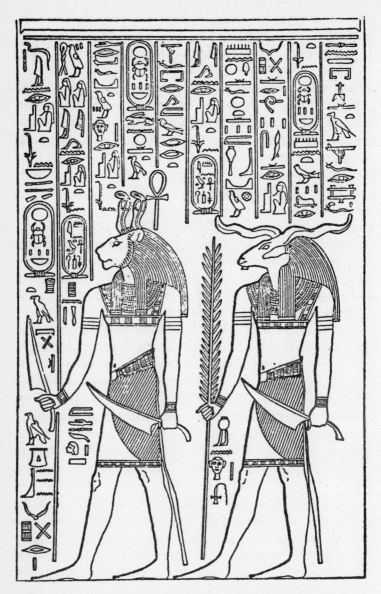

Six fearsome genies, armed with knives and having the heads of a ram, a crocodile, a lion and a man. They stand in the path of the traveller who travels the Netherworld and kill him without pity if he is ignorant of the

names and numbers. On the other hand, if the traveller proves his
knowledge, they become his assistants in the battle which he will wage
against the darkness.

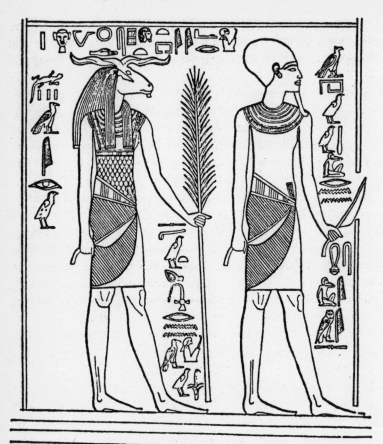

against the necromancers and black magicians. He breaks their
pens, tears up their archives. Thus he preserves his head, and his
bones stay joined together.[15] Because he is a skilful scribe, the
magician is particularly suited to handling the pen. He follows
the precise instructions given by his masters: 'You will draw
every adversary of Re, and every adversary of the pharaoh living
or dead, and every outlaw he can think of, the names of their
fathers, mothers and children—each one of them, writing them
with fresh ink on a papyrus leaf which has never been used—
their names being written on their chests, they themselves being

fashioned in wax, and bound with ties of black thread; they are spat upon, ground under the left foot, struck with the knife and the spear and thrown upon the fire in the blacksmith's furnace.[16]

The Enemy is everywhere. On the field of battle, the pharaoh's enemies are not merely human. They are possessed by a hostile force against which the pharaoh must use magical weapons. Before any battle, he must proceed to put a spell on his enemies, part of the official techniques of war practised by the State. The sacred model for this is supplied by the rituals which the priests celebrate in the temples for the purpose of fighting the enemies of the Light. In non-religious matters it is used to combat Egypt's attackers and safeguard its frontiers. Lists of enemies are written in red ink on clay figurines which represent enemies who have been conquered and fettered. These figurines are struck, pierced, spat upon and burnt. This magical annihilation is the underlying reason for the portrayal of enemies as eternally cast down on the walls of the temples or on the plinths of royal statues.[17]

The breaking of vases which had been filled with evil power was a State magical rite. In many places in Egypt, pieces of pottery are to be found broken into several pieces. Thus the hostile forces are scattered. This technique, which was passed down from the earliest times, was practised throughout Egyptian history. In the Middle Kingdom particularly, the names of enemies were written on vases and cups—enemy princes and chiefs were the main adversaries shown. Thanks to the magicians, gods and spirits intervened. So that no one should be overlooked the names of negro princes were also noted, indicating, for safety's sake: 'All the negroes, their strong men, their runners, their allies, their confederates who will be hostile, throughout the whole land.' They do not forget to include in this magic list the Palestinians, the Libyans and even the men and women of Egypt who might conspire within the borders.

Amongst his enemies the magician includes 'all evil words, all evil thoughts, all evil intrigues, all evil struggles, all evil quarrels, all evil designs, all evil things, all evil dreams.'[18] Nothing can beat professional thoroughness.

At Mirgissa, a site at the level of the second cataract of the Nile, on the western bank, numerous objects were found which bear curses, statues of prisoners, vases and pottery. The princes of foreign lands were regarded as evil beings who were in rebellion against the harmony of the world.[19] Evil exists; it must be exorcised. It is also the best way to establish an impassable frontier.

For the experienced magician who has freed himself from suffering like the risen Osiris, it is possible to conquer the Enemy and crush him beneath his sandals. That is why his actions are effective when he utters the right words over a wax figurine.[20] Some people have wondered if these were 'golems'—animated creatures. In fact these figurines do not move. They are condemned to inertia, so that inertia will strike the person whom one wishes to attack.

One warning which should be respected is to behead the enemy in wax, the enemy drawn on a papyrus or carved in wood.[21] Thus the inhabitants of the desert will not revolt against Egypt, there will be neither war nor rebellion in the land, the king will be obeyed, the land of the gods will be defended.

The magician enters the Enemy's stomach as a fly, turns his face to the back of his head, and puts his feet on backwards. He weakens him, empties him of his substance.[22] He evokes the power of the bull god Montu and that of Seth. He takes earth in his right hand and recites a spell over it. He breaks the enemy's bones and devours his flesh. He tears his power from him to take possession of it.[23]

The adversary's attack translates into precise physical phenomena, thus—catalepsy. Then the magician takes an ass's head and places it between his feet, facing the rising sun and again at the end of the day. He anoints his right foot with a substance made from a Syrian stone, thus foreshadowing the modern lithotherapy, and the left foot with clay. He anoints his hands with ass's blood. He must repeat the spells for seven days, knotting palm fibres in his hand, round his phallus and round his head. He invokes the power which is in the air, invisible.[24] Thus he conquers catalepsy and death.

The magician uses charms to obtain a meeting with a powerful man who would refuse to parley with him. He only needs to declare that he is carrying the mummy of Osiris to Abydos. If the enemy should persist he would be beaten.[25]

Threats

To ensure that he can really master the world of the gods, both good and bad, favourable or unfavourable, the magician does not hesitate to use threats. In Chapter 219 of the *Pyramid Texts* the king identifies himself with Osiris, and each god in turn. To each he says, 'If the god lives, the king will live; if the god does not die, the king will not die.' They were content in early times to link the fate of the pharaoh with that of the gods by magic. But the magician goes further. He can use the secret name of a god, that of Shu for example, to change the order of things. If he should pronounce it on the bank of a river it would dry up. If it were spoken on the land it would catch fire. If the crocodile should attack the magician, the south would change into the north, and the world would tilt.

Worse still, violent insults are addressed to gods and goddesses, especially in Chapter 534 of the *Pyramid Texts*, whose words are intended to prevent the coming of Osiris, Horus, Seth the castrated, dribbling Khenty-Irty, Thoth the motherless, Isis, swollen with putrescence, Nephthys, concubine without a vagina. Horrible descriptions that drag the noble gods in the mud.

When the magician makes terrible threats against the gods he takes one important precaution: 'It is not I who speaks thus,' he adds, 'nor I who repeats that, but really the magic force which has come to attack the one with whom I am concerned.'[26] In that way, the miracle-worker can speak terrifying words which summon up the worst—for example setting fire to Busiris and burning Osiris.

Magical threats are used to heal. If someone who is gravely ill is in danger of dying, the magician uses this ultimate weapon: 'If the poison spreads through the body,' he threatens, 'if it ventures into any part of the body, there will be no offerings laid upon the offering tables in the temples, no water will be poured over the altars, no fire will be lit in a sacrificial table, no piece of meat will be taken to the temple. But if the poison falls to earth, all the temples will be overjoyed, the gods will be happy in their sanctuaries.'[27]

The State itself does not hesitate to use this procedure. A royal decree ordains that all inauspicious influences and all kinds of death shall be averted. If the magic were not effective the reprisals would be dreadful—no more water for the one who is in the sarcophagus; the one who is in Abydos, that is, Osiris, would not be buried; there would be no more offerings for the one who is in Heliopolis, meaning the god Re.[28] The forces of evil know where to stop.

The gods take similar precautions. Horus, according to some traditions, has a wife. Like many others she dreads being bitten by reptiles. But 'if Horus' wife was bitten, the flood would not water the banks; the sun would not be allowed to shine on the earth, nor would the grain be allowed to grow; it would not be possible to make bread, nor to brew the pitchers of beer for the three hundred and fifty-five gods who would go hungry night and day.'[29]

When the magician appeals to the gods and claims their assistance, they cannot refuse him. He directly threatens the symbolic animals in whom they are incarnated, thereby 'forcing their hand'. In strong terms he addresses each divine power who is affected: 'If you do not listen to my words I will cut the head off a cow on Hathor's forecourt, I will decapitate a hippopotamus on the forecourt of Seth, I shall make Anubis sit wrapped in a dog's skin and Seth sit wrapped in a crocodile skin.'[30]

The same sort of threat is made to magical objects like the lantern which accompanies the divine presence. The magician orders it to submit to him when Osiris is in his ship with Isis at his head and Nephthys at his feet. The lantern must intervene on behalf of the magician or he will deprive it of oil.

The Dangers of the Night

The magician goes out at night, in the darkness, with Horus in front of him and Seth at his right hand. He is charged with a message from the great gods. Accompanied in this way he does not fear the demons that prowl in the shadows. The dead cannot disturb him. It is he who threatens them: he can cut off their hands, blind their eyes, close their mouths. 'I am Horus-Seth,' he proclaims, thus creating an extraordinary union, beyond duality, beyond 'good' or 'evil'.[31]

The night is dangerous. Spectres hide in it to circle the earth. These are the ghosts, the wandering dead. The magician protects himself by declaring that he is the master of the universe. He is the young god, lord of Truth and justice. In his role as companion of the Creator, Atum, he roams the sky and knows its pathways.[32]

Anyone who goes out at night takes precautions. He carries a special light and arms himself with protective serpents. Evil will not attack him.[33] The light is placed inside the magician's eyes so that he can replace night with day and travel the earth, leaving the horizon of the sky, without dying anew. He looks upon Re, sees the light face to face.[34]

There is a special book to drive away the fears that cripple a man during the night. He must look up, awaken his spiritual qualities. So will he perceive the Master of All. He must recite the spells over a piece of fine linen which he wraps round his throat to keep himself calm.[35]

The magician has an arsenal of weapons against nightmares. He mocks the demons who disturb his sleep. He appeals to the divinities who are present in the barque of the night that crosses the sky. He paints pictures of guardian spirits on the bedhead, and writes magic spells on it. Against bad dreams, the magician summons by his will a good dream, a night which would be like day. The evils roused by Seth are driven off. Like Re, the magician will be victorious over his enemies who emerge from the shadows. He will use herbs steeped in beer and myrrh. He will rub the face of the sleeper to dispel nightmares.[36] He speaks these potent words: 'See, this is the Master of All, and this is

Those-who-exist. This is Atum, this is Wadjet, the mistress of terror in the great barque, this is the child, this is the master of Truth, this is the face of Atum on the upper road, this is the devouring flame which has been created by Sha, the lord of the skies.'[37] These apparitions frighten the demons. The just man sleeps in peace, protected by magic.

8 Magic and Medicine

The night in Luxor is never dark. Doubtless demons only exist for those who fear them. But illness certainly exists. Often it strikes us when we least expect it. My hosts, a magical family if ever there was one, knew a fair amount about Western medicine. They did not have much faith in it. Egyptian doctors trained in London and Paris had tried in vain to convince them. 'When one treats an illness in the wrong way,' the father explained to me, 'one does not destroy its roots. At best one displaces it. At worst one makes it grow.' Magic plus Medicine, is that the proper path?

A Doctor Magician

Magical medicine was probably born in Egypt. It is not an artificial creation, but a science both theoretical and experimental at the same time, which has as its basic criterion the wish to maintain the human body in harmony with the cosmos, so that it will serve as a receptacle for the vital forces which created the universe. Anyone affected by an illness, suffering or pain is the prey of a negative force, a hostile divinity, or even of a demon. The doctor magician must treat the cause, not the effect, then attack the invisible and irrational power which is disturbing the system.

An important fact to be established in understanding the principles of magical medicine is that it carries no moral overtones. The healing god is not 'good', the aggressive god is not 'bad'. They are both expressions of the creative force which circulates everywhere. It is the human being who reacts either harmoniously or inharmoniously to his surroundings; it is he who accepts and manipulates the divinities who rule his existence 'well' or 'badly'.

Today, we put magic and medicine in opposition to each other. The Egyptians preferred to unite the two techniques to attain a science of man which was much more complete and much more vast. We must remember, after all, that present-day branches of medicine, which are exclusively based on chemical and mathematical reasoning, train doctors some of whom end by questioning the value of their practices. Healing is an art as much as a science, a magic of being as much as a rational analysis.

Egyptian medicine was hidden beneath secret signs whose mysteries only the 'philosophers', those who love wisdom, could understand. The mystery was nevertheless written down and passed on, in particular in the Egyptian papyri and Arabic books of spells, translated into Latin and passed from practitioner to practitioner until the fifteenth century, especially in the German courts which still had knowledge of some of the secrets of the Egyptian priests.

It is magic which gives medicine its immunising qualities. It prevents the illness from getting near the body. The doctor prepares his medications scientifically. But he judges that this science is not enough. A magic spell must be added to give it a soul. Although some medicines are simple, most of them are complex and treat the patients who have been attacked by demons. When the illness persists, it is because Seth or some other demon has crossed the patient's path and attacked him. It makes him impure. Whence the need for the intervention of the magician, the '*waab-priest*' of Sekhmet who is trained to heal.

Illnesses are caused by male or female enemies against whom the magician fights as a warrior. The instruments he uses are like weapons. One does not become a doctor-magician without a long and difficult initiation which, for the masters of the guild, took place in Heliopolis. In the presence of the mother of the gods from whom he receives blessings, the student learns the incantations laid down by the Master of the Universe himself when he drives off the harmful forces. The first precept is: 'God gives life to the one he loves.'

To be better able to help the patient recover his health, the magician assumes the likeness of certain divinities, first and foremost Re. He informs the divinities of this: 'O Re, Geb, Nut, Osiris, Horus! Make well the heart of this suffering man! Lead him back to life as you made the heart of Re revive during the attack by Nehaher (a demon)! Drive out the poison that is in his body as you banished the venom of Apophis which was in the body of the great god!' The inescapable conclusion for the patient is that 'Re is your protection.'[1]

An essential step is to speak to the demon directly so that he will reveal his evil intentions and the way he is disabling the one he has possessed. 'Back,' says the magician, 'enemy, demon who brings this trouble upon another! You say that you inflict these wounds on this head which is his, to force your way into his forehead which is his, to crush his temples which are his! Go, retreat before the crushing power of that blazing eye which is his! He wards off your aggressive power, he scatters your ejaculations, your seed, your nuisances, the products of your digestion, your oppressions, your evils, your torments, your inflammations, your afflictions, heat and fire, all the evil things of which you said, "he will suffer because of them."' Thanks to Re, the patient remains alive. The sun god stops the poisons from killing him.

But Re himself is not totally protected from the assault of evil forces. His barque may be brought to a halt in the sky. With the cosmic voyage interrupted, the universe stops because Horus is in danger. The patient is identified with Horus, so the human being as well as the god must be freed from their ills, so that order can be re-established in the universe.[2]

Horus' protection is provided by the Elder in the sky who governs all that is, the great dwarf who goes round the *Duat*, the world between, the book of the night which travels in the mountain of the west, the great hidden power, the immense falcon which flies in the sky, on the earth and in the *Duat*, the sacred scarab, the secret body symbolised by the mummy, the divine phoenix, Horus' own name, the names of his father Osiris, his images in his nomes, the lamentation of his mother Isis: these likewise protect the sick man who has been identified with Horus when he is properly cared for by a magician.

In one case which appears to be unique, a sick man was advised to speak directly to the *Duat*,[3] in other words to that particular world which is neither sky nor earth and surrounds the universe. This is a rarity, for the magician is the essential intermediary between the illness and its cause. To learn his craft, he can use oral instruction given by the Houses of Life and written teaching, the medical papyri.

These are not available to all and sundry. The *London Medical Papyrus*, for example, is not a secular document. It was found, one night, in a temple room. A moonbeam illuminated it and it was then taken to the king. This great event occurred whilst the Ennead were conferring. Every medical document really belongs in the domain of sacred things.

This marvellous art, which is of divine origin, requires close cooperation between the doctor and his patient. Expertise alone is not enough. The effect of the medicine is only given full play if the will to exorcise the evil also comes from the heart and body of the sick man. The magic spell helps to put the joint action of the sick man and his healer into concrete form. Just as Horus and Seth became 'healthy', the first provided with a new eye, the second with new testicles, so the man who is on earth can enjoy physical wholeness by recovering his health.[4]

The doctor-magician, a man who has been initiated and is knowledgeable, has an impressive therapeutic arsenal at his disposal. To root out the evil from the patient's body he has the benefit of his technical knowledge, of the magical identification of his patient with a god (it is often Horus fighting Seth), of knowledge of the names of the enemies and of the demons, of his ability to talk to the evil power to persuade it of its weakness, and of the power within the sick person who has the resources within himself to fight and overcome. If the illness has unfortunately penetrated very deeply into the body, there remains the possibility of challenging it, threatening it, commanding it to be gone, driving it out. The magician explains to the illness that it will be ill at ease in the parts of the body where it wishes to go:

the tongue will be a serpent to it, the anus will disgust it, the teeth will pulverise it. There is no doubt that the illness would feel much more at ease in its own dwelling place, far from humans.

In Heliopolis, as we have seen, the doctor-magician underwent a long and difficult initiation. So harsh that he had to cure himself before being able to heal others. Must we conclude from this information[6] that the trainee was infected with an illness in order to establish how self-possessed and knowledgeable he was? Or had he 'simply' passed the physical tests which are always part of a ritual of initiation? Whatever the case, the new doctor, after this probationary period, visited the other Houses of Life, such as the one at Sais, and received teaching from many colleagues. The major divinities assisted in this task. Re in person defended him from enemies both visible and invisible. His guide was Thoth, he who knows the spells and teaches them to the students so that they may free from evil those whom the god wishes to keep alive.

The first duty of the magician is to bind the destiny of the sick man to that of the universe. If he is not healed, the sky will fall, the light disappear. The demon who causes this disharmony will himself be wiped out by the catastrophe. To save himself he has no alternative but to flee ... which is the same thing as the healing of his victim.

An important point is that the taking of medicine is compared to the opening of the mouth by the gods Ptah and Sokaris during the rites of resurrection. The magic spell was recited by Nephthys, 'the mistress of the temple'. The purpose of the opening of the mouth was to bring the mummy to life and animate the statue. By practising this 'operation' on a sick man, one gives him an immense vital potential and the ability to resist attacks from outside. When one takes a remedy it is necessary to pronounce the magic words. The two actions reinforce one another. The matter from which the medicine is made is given life by the spell.[7]

To take off a bandage, Horus, who was delivered by Isis from the evil done to him by Seth, is evoked. The sick man implores

Isis, 'the Great one of Magic', to remove from him all evil influences. He has entered the fire, he has left the water, he will not let himself fall into the demons' traps.[8] The magician says, 'Unbound he was, unbound he was by Isis. Unbound was Horus by Isis from all the evil done to him by his brother Seth, when he killed his father Osiris. O Isis, great magician, unbind me, deliver me from all evil, harmful and red things, from a god's illness and from a goddess's illness, from male death and from female death, from male and female enemies who will come against me.'[9]

No medical act, however simple, is seen as a purely material act. It is always linked to the world of magic in which it finds a divine model. The powers of the Egyptian doctors were often surprising, even in the light of modern knowledge. Egyptologists have often belittled the spell in the *Edwin Smith medical papyrus* which proposes to 'transform an old man into a young man twenty years old', but it seems certain that the wise men of Egypt practised a science of transmutation and rejuvenation which explains the longevity of some rulers, however weighed down with duties and work. Was not the traditional age of the wise men one hundred and ten years?

A text in the *Ebers papyrus* alludes to a fundamental aspect of Egyptian knowledge—perception of reality by intuition from the heart: 'the beginning of the secret of the doctor, knowledge of the heart's movements and knowledge of the heart. There are vessels within it which go to all the limbs. Wherever the practitioner puts his fingers, on the head, neck, hands or the heart itself, the arms, legs or wherever this may be, he will feel there something of the heart, for its vessels go to each limb; that is why it speaks in the vessels of each limb.'

This is not a matter, as has often been supposed, of elementary physiology, but on the contrary, of exact information about the person's 'insubstantial body' which must be tended with as much care as the physical body. Following the same patterns of thought, and holding to a logic of magic, the magician only uses physical or direct remedies against poison, for example. He makes seven knots in some material, holds a relic in his hands from a chest

The genie Nedj-Her, seated, crowned and holding Life in its hands. The initiate must know how to reply to the questions set by his guardian of the threshold to discover that life within himself.

kept in Heliopolis which contains, in particular, a seal of black stone. Is not the knowledge of secret names the most effective remedy against malignant humours?[10] Faced with such evil, only magic can fight with any chance of success. If the patient is badly affected, the doctor will bestow upon him a terrible rage which will make him capable of destroying cities like Busiris and Mendes, of preventing the offerings reaching Abydos, in brief of disturbing the order of the world. The demons of the illness will be forced to retreat.

To combat fever and catarrh the remedy is . . . a royal decree! The king of Upper and Lower Egypt, Osiris, tells his vizier, the hereditary prince Geb, to step the mast of his ship, raise the sail and voyage to the field of reeds. He must lead the hostile forces, fever and catarrh, far from the earth. These divine words are to be spoken over two divine barques and two complete eyes; two scarabs are drawn on papyrus which will be placed on the patient's throat.[11]

For a cold, an infection which seems to have been particularly distressing to the Egyptians, the doctor-magician uses all his power of eloquence: 'Begone, coryza, son of coryza! You who breaks bones, who shatters the skull, who digs into the brain, who makes ill the seven orifices of the head, servants of Re, praise-singers of Thoth. See, I have brought the remedy against you, the potion for you—the milk of a woman who has given birth to a male child, and perfumed resin. This is to be said four times over the milk of a woman who has given birth to a male child and over sweet-smelling resin. To be placed in the nostril.'[12]

Quite trivial incidents often have disastrous consequences: thus there is a magic spell to prevent a man who has a bone wedged in his throat from choking. The magician identifies himself with a lion's breast, a ram's head and a leopard's tooth. His treatment is to pour oil down the patient's throat. He helps him swallow the oil with his finger. When he coughs up his saliva the bone will come with it.[13] For the same thing, the magician, using means apparently out of all proportion to the problem, takes on the identity of the one whose head touches the sky and whose feet rest upon the eternal waters. A falcon's egg in his mouth and an ibis' egg in his stomach are needed.

The bone of a god, man, bird, animal or fish will leave the patient's mouth and fall into the hand of the magician, son of the living god.

Saliva is an excellent remedy. By spitting onto a wound one may heal it. Saliva is one of those secretions and exudations which, like blood, sweat and urine, come from the bodies of the gods. That is why the use of excrement, urine and other substances which are at first sight repugnant, is derived from a magical concept. The world of the demonic forces is the inverse of that of the just man. The damned in the other world eat excrement and hang their heads as they go. Nevertheless, the homeopathic use of these natural substances is possible. Like other elements of life, they contain a small part of the divinity which the magician must know how to extract and use. A late legacy of this idea, a curious tradition which comes from Egypt, lasted into the Middle Ages and was known until the seventeenth century. To determine the sex of the unborn baby, spelt and wheat are soaked in the urine of the pregnant woman and the grains placed in two sachets. If the wheat germinates, a boy will be born. If the spelt, a girl. Another method is to dig two ditches. Barley is thrown into one, wheat into the other. Then the pregnant woman's urine is poured into both and covered with earth. If the wheat sprouts more quickly than the barley it will be a boy. But if the barley comes up first, the mother will give birth to a girl.[14]

These magical anecdotes, which are nevertheless based on chemical knowledge, must not mask those extraordinary aspects of State magic such as the healing statues. These, covered in magic texts and consecrated in the temples, were placed in the sacred sanatoriums or in chapels. Their bases were hollowed out into a basin in which the water collected which was poured over the statue and which, in passing over the sacred texts, was impregnated with magic. Such water, which had acquired energy, was offered to the sick or those unfortunate enough to be stung by a serpent or scorpion. This magic water also had protective qualities, safeguarding travellers who ventured into the desert from all attack.

Blood and Magic

In every known kind of magic, blood plays some role. It carries vital qualities which are most important, whose secrets are only penetrated by an experienced magician. That is why blood is an ingredient of several products. We know, for example, of an ointment made from the blood of a black calf and with it the horn of a black bull, a product which gives energy to the user.

Is not Pharaoh himself of the blood of Re,[15] the blood of the sun?

*A star-goddess receives energy from the sun which enters her mouth. She
passes it on to a serpent, symbol of the earthly powers, who are thus
brought to life by a celestial energy. That which is above is as that which is
below.*

Now, it is Re himself who opens the body of the sick man
and leads him back to life, preventing the poisons from
taking effect, and not leaving him to the mercy of the noxious
fluids. The magic words are to be spoken over a figure of
Re drawn with the blood of an *abdju* fish on a piece of royal
linen, which is then placed on the head of the individual
concerned.[16]

When the goddess Sekhmet breaks free, ready to destroy
humanity, Re is forced to intervene. The goddess is made to drink
a magical brew the colour of blood. Although this is a delicate

operation, if it succeeds fully then the furious Sekhmet changes into the gentle Hathor.

Blood and sweat are mingled in a spell of regeneration designed to increase the power of the magician: 'May the sweat of the gods reach you, may Re's protection spread over your body, may you have access to the sacred land, to the sacred soil in the country places, may you do what you wish in the Two Lands, thanks to the divine sweat which comes from the land of Punt. May the grease of your enemies reach you, may your heart be regenerated thanks to the blood of those who rebel against you!'[17]

The blood of the goddess Isis protects the magician from all negative attacks, and prevents anyone from doing evil to him. Feminine blood is also the blood of defloration; exceptional qualities were attributed to it,[18] linked to the revelation of the secret names of the gods, and to the acquisition of the power to overwhelm evil beings. In a way the magician, in the practice of his art, was making love to a goddess who was always virgin and who revealed to him her eternal truth.

An over-simple magic degrades this symbolism by using a mixture of blood and sperm to release the passion of love in the breast of a desired person. Love, even on the simplest level, is a common vibration between two different energies—hence the intervention of magicians who bless such unions.

Blood is a precious liquid. That is why a haemorrhage is considered to be a dreadful evil. Happily there is a spell to stop it: 'Be gone, you who are on the hand of Horus! Be gone, you who are on the hand of Seth! The flowing blood is stopped!' The spell is recited over an amulet in the form of a bed, which is then placed on the behind of the individual concerned.[19]

Haemorrhage in women is one of the most serious ills. To stop it one invokes Anubis who prevented the flood from spreading over that which is pure. The spells are spoken over the threads of a piece of material tied in a knot. Then it is placed inside the sick woman's vagina.[20] While fasting, she may also be made to drink the juice of the plant called 'Great Nile', mixed with beer.[21] The flow of the river is compared to the menstrual flow. Both must be regular if the land of men like the woman's body is to be in harmony.

Headaches

The head must be safeguarded from illness for it contains the doors of life: the eyes to see and recreate the world, the nose to breathe the insubstantial as well as the material, the ears to hear the Word and speech, the mouth so that the man may live.[22] Headaches, which disturb this major 'organ', even affected Horus, who climbed a mountain in summer at midday. He found the gods holding a banquet in a judgement chamber. They invited him to share their repast. But Horus replied that he had no appetite. He was suffering from a migraine. He was burning with fever. Would the three hundred and sixty-five gods seated at the banquet please relieve the pain in his head! The magician must tell this story seven times whilst he treats a sick man, rubbing his hands, body and feet with a special ointment.[23]

Another tale describes Horus, still with a migraine, passing a day lying on a cushion. Seth, his brother, watches over him. The resourceful magician has acquired the material from which the cushion had been cut and made seven knots in it. He applies them to the big toe of the patient he is treating.[24] Horus, for his part, appealed to Isis and suggested a radical remedy—that the goddess should give him her head in place of his own. Isis did not agree to this most delicate of courses. However, she did do something to help Horus, making magic knots, always seven in number.[25] The magician imitates the goddess and applies the material to the left foot of the patient for, concludes the spell, 'that which has been applied to the lower parts is good for the upper parts.' How can we fail to see here one of the roots of that famous hermetic saying, 'that which is above is like that which is below, and that which is below is like that which is above'?

It is a wise precaution to carry in the form of an amulet the head of one of certain divinities (Bes or Hathor, for example) to represent the entire pantheon. The capitals called 'Hathoric'—in other words the giant heads of the goddess—which surmount the columns of some temples, such as the one at Dendera, are very potent talismen which protect the building.

The sick man's head is identified with that of Re. That is why there will be cosmic disasters if the patient doesn't recover his health. Re's head gives light to the world and life to mankind. It is therefore important that Re does not go to sleep hungry, and that the gods are not sad. Otherwise we risk seeing the return of that primordial darkness, that time, before creation, when the skies were one. The heavenly water would be stripped from the earth which would be condemned to sterility. Clearly, the consequences of not treating a divine migraine by magic would be terrifying.

If the pain affects both sides of the head, it is because a demon has made a feast of his victim. The position is grave. A mask must be procured for the sick man made by the ram god Khnum. Once he is identified with the god, the patient receives the power to vanquish the evil. But there are simpler remedies which will get rid of a persistent migraine. Isis has given us an example. She let down her hair like a woman in mourning, in an analogy with the disorder of Horus' hair, who was struck by Seth whilst they fought. He who puts his hair in order will avoid headaches.[26]

Another recommendation is to put one's hands on one's head— the pains will disappear under the effect of the magnetism which one can give onself, on condition that the magical act allows one to take the identity of Horus the Elder with his primeval vigour. It is a useful precaution also to cover the upper part of the shoulder and the vertebrae with an amulet, a sort of protective wig like that woven and bound by Isis and Nephthys.

Another way of combating migraine is to recite a spell over a clay crocodile in whose mouth a seed has been placed. On the figurine's head should be a faience eye. One must then bind it and draw a picture of the gods on a band of linen.[27]

Another effective charm is to treat the sick man's head like that of Osiris Onophris, on whose head were placed 377 divine serpents which spat flames and put evil to flight.[28] The magician goes on the attack by throwing into the fire the animal from the Netherworld, whose forepart resembles that of a jackal and who

has put a curse on the patient. By destroying the cause he annihilates the effect.

It is particularly important to keep one's head. Osiris' head
was an important relic, kept near Abydos, the principal cult centre
of the god. By becoming Osiris, the just man acquires divine
status. But he avoids having his head cut off. He takes every
precaution to keep it intact in the kingdom of the dead.[29] To
reduce any risk, people even plan for 'replacement heads' to
place in their tombs.

Chapter 101 of the *Coffin Texts* is one of the strangest texts.
The magician recites it over a head placed on the soil, lit by the
light cast from a window. The purpose of this operation is a
psychical transmigration. The human soul gains the ability to
move around the cosmos and meet Shu, the god of the shining
air. In the head are hidden mysterious powers which only the
magician can awaken and bring to maturity. This ancient knowledge has been preserved in the West, notably in the masonic
rituals. It is worth noting, for example, that the Apprentice who
perjures himself and betrays the secrets has his throat cut symbolically—he loses his head and the sense of living in spirit.

Stomach aches

The gods are not spared this unhappy affliction from which divinities as important as Horus and Re suffered. When the sun-god
complains of pains in his stomach the barque stops. Its heavenly
journey is interrupted. The crew is worried, for when the voyage
stops the order of the world is in peril. An appeal must be made
to the great ones at Heliopolis, meaning the masters of magic
who know the most complicated remedies. To soothe the patient,
he is magnetised by placing a hand on his stomach. At the same
time, a spell is recited over a clay statue of a woman into which
the magician sends the evil.[30] Appeal is made to the *Duat* across
the surface of the earth. The sky, the world between and the
earth are placed in peril when Re has abdominal pains. The very
movement of the stars is in danger of ceasing, like the barque.

Stomach ache is caused by a demon. Isis and Nephthys must

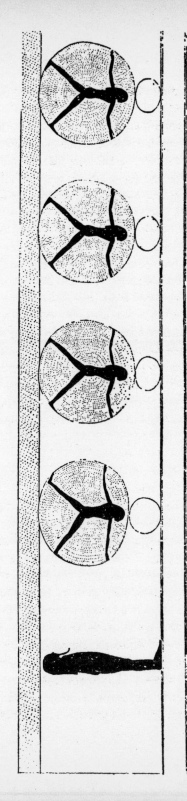

Representations of people hanging upside down, spreadeagled inside a circle. This is the world inverted, where everything 'turns' in the opposite way to harmony. Knowledge of magic and of the spells of life permit the initiate to avoid this position, correct the situation and remain upright throughout the universe.

be consulted. Isis asks if it is caused by worms. If that is the case, nineteen signs are carved with the point of a harpoon. Magic words must be spoken over the stomach of the sick man.[31]

Horus complains of stomach ache because he has eaten a golden fish from Re's pure lake. He has thus broken a taboo. The spell must be recited over a disk of yellow ochre. Then, anoint the sick man with honey and wash him.[32]

Horus has committed an even graver crime. He has eaten a falcon, his own sacred animal. The consequences are not long in coming. He writhes with pain. The pain bores into his stomach. He appeals to demons to warn his mother Isis. But they have great difficulty in finding one swift enough to cross space. At last, he chooses one who sails on the breeze and returns in the same way. The demon warns Isis that Horus is in pain. The goddess evokes her true name which leads the sun to the west and the moon to the east and raises the three hundred veins which surround the navel, along with any illness afflicting the patient's body. Horus is saved. But the Coptic magic papyrus which relates this story finishes in a very strange fashion, the spell concluding with these words: 'I who speak, I am the Lord Jesus who heals.' Christ has undoubtedly inherited the magic power of the Great Isis.

The Eye and the Ear

There are many spells to protect the eyes. The desert wind causes ophthalmia and cataracts, illnesses carried by demons. Now the eye is a vital organ. The word 'to create' in Egyptian is written with an eye. To see is to recreate, to open oneself to reality. The eye of the flesh is the material expression of an inner eye. The healthy eye, the complete eye, are symbols of wholeness, of life in its fullness. that is why the magician accomplishes a creative act in regenerating, by the use of the eye, one who shows himself worthy of initiation into the mysteries: 'I have applied the Eye of Horus to you so that your face may be regenerated by it, I have anointed your eyes with the green ointment and the black ointment so that your face may be regenerated by them . . . I complete your face with ointment from the Eye of Horus, by which it was completed. He reattaches your bones, he reassembles your limbs, he reunites your flesh and scatters your ills.'[33]

To combat eye troubles, the magician recalls a disorder of the cosmos which occurred one evening in the northern sky and the southern sky. One of the pillars which support the heavens fell into the water. To prevent the collapse of the universe, the magician fixes the heads of the crew of Re's ship firmly on their shoulders. They will be fit to carry out their duties and the boat will sail normally. These words are to be spoken over the gall bladder of a tortoise mixed with honey. This product is applied to the outside of the eyes.[34]

It is said that the treatment of eye troubles has a direct connection with the equilibrium of the universe. Another proof of this is that one appeals to the Eye of Horus in treating eye troubles. It destroys troubles caused by malign spirits, by dead men and women, by male and female enemies.[35] It is thanks to the Eye of Horus that any remedy applied to both eyes proves effective. It was prepared specially by the master magicians of Heliopolis. Thoth was charged with leading the Eye into the Great House which is in the holy city and he protects it from all harmful influences.[36]

If, despite these precautions, a leucoma occurs, a voice reverberates in the southern sky. The northern sky is troubled. A building collapses, the stones fall into the water. This problem that threatens to bring ruin must be put right, the building must be repaired. Thus, evil is driven back and the eye is saved.[37]

To carry the eye as an amulet allows one to have the measure of all things upon one's person, a parallel with the Eye of Re who annihilates his enemies. 'The Eye of Horus' is also the generic name for an offering—the man who wears it as an amulet thereby offers himself to the god, he makes a gift of his person to the Creator and thus saves himself from evil.

In Egypt the Eye is everywhere, for those who can see it. It is carved on sarcophagi, on stelae, on boats. In every place it is the eye from beyond which observes the living and guides them. The king, as ever, provides an example. The uraeus, the female serpent which he wears on his brow, is 'the burning eye of Re', the potent fire of the crown which scatters his adversaries. At Saqqara, in the funerary domain of king Djoser, a frieze of uraei serves as eyes protecting the soul of the pharaoh. The same is true of the two serpents which encircle the sun, making a symbol that is often drawn on temple walls. The *Stela of Metternich* speaks also of the divine eye of the right and the divine eye of the left. Thus with the creator's gaze upon the whole world, the stars are held in their place and time unrolls as it should, giving humanity its proper role in creation.

The magician paints an eye on his hand. Inside the eye is the image of the god Onouris whose name means 'He who brings that which is far off', that is, the goddess who symbolises the eye which fled into far countries and which the magician must bring back to Egypt.[38] By pronouncing the spells over an eye of lapis-lazuli, the magician states that he is able to make any one of his limbs see and thus make it clairvoyant.[39]

Magic spells pronounced over the complete eye, the *wedjat* bearing the figure of Onouris, authorise the magician to declare: 'I am a being chosen from a multitude, who has left the *Duat*, whose name is unknown. If his name is spoken on the bank of a river, it will dry up. If his name is spoken on the earth, it will put forth a flame. I am Shu, symbol of the Light, who sits inside the complete eye of his father. If something which is on the water opens its mouth, if it moves its arms, I will make the earth be invaded by the flood, so that the south becomes the north and the earth be turned upside down.'

When the magician uses a vase to measure, this is not a secular object but a 'relic' which was once used to measure the Eye of Horus. But that Eye is also a magical means by which Horus resuscitated Osiris.

It is said that the biologist, chemist and alchemist of Egypt had the 'good eye' to make calculations and find the right proportions in the composition of medicines and drugs. This 'good eye' sees its work thwarted by an 'evil eye' which gives the magician a lot of trouble. The dragon Apophis turns his evil eye against Re. He hypnotises the crew of the solar barque. Only

Seth can resist for he himself possesses a formidable gaze which enables him to combat the evil dragon. He, like the other powers of darkness, seeks to injure or steal the Eye of Re. The only solution is to blind Apophis to stop him doing harm. If he cannot see, he will not be able to spread unhappiness. The exact method for doing this is laid down in the rite of hitting the ball. In this game against Apophis, pharaoh strikes a ball in the presence of the goddess Hathor. The ball is the eye of the dragon Apophis, which is thus damaged so that the life of the cosmos can continue in harmony. This rite forms part of a series of magical actions which consist of killing the oryx, the crocodile, the tortoise and offering the sacrifices for the defeat of an evil being; there are many means of mastering negative forces by using their own energy.[40]

From ancient times, a serpent's gaze was considered to be dangerous. The cobra, which still hides today in the crannies of the temple walls, was sometimes reputed to have a hypnotic gaze. Actually the sight of this fearsome reptile is so impressive that it roots one to the spot. That is when, if no precautions are taken to protect the eyes, the cobra spits its venom and blinds its victim. This jet of venom is as formidable as a bite, for it can cause permanent blindness.

It is better not to come face to face with evil beings; that is why the magician, with his art, makes them look behind them.

The ear deserves the magician's attention just as much. The ears, in effect, are the doors by which breath enters, sometimes as life (by the right ear) and sometimes as death (by the left ear). Care must be taken that a person is not violated or impregnated by negative energies which could enter the ears at any moment and reach the heart. It is best to be a 'good listener'—that is, one who listens only to pleasant sounds. It is also essential to identify the evil genies who try to penetrate the ear duct.

On a stela dedicated to the god Min, shown as 'bull of his mother', a worshipper is seen kneeling and making a gesture of adoration to ithyphallic Amun-Min. Above him are two gigantic ears.[41] This is the assurance that the god will hear his prayer and answer. In the Late Dynastic Period these 'stelae with ears' proliferated, bearing the most desperate pleas. The believers were confident that their prayers would be granted through sympathetic magic which would draw the attention of the gods to their plight.

A Heavenly Food

What the pharaoh hates is hunger. He will not eat it. What he also hates is thirst. He will not drink it.[42] This implies that the sovereign may be satisfied only by very special food. The officials of the mouth, as in ancient China, held an enviable rank at court. The quality and quantity of the food and drink are equally important, for the living as for the dead. In the tombs 'Notices of the offerings' are displayed, actual menus meant for the inhabitants of the other world. It is not the material part of these provisions that matters, but their essence which emanates from the hieroglyphs themselves when the offering spells are intoned. Thus it is the magic of the Word which really nourishes the souls of the dwellers in the underworld. The classic formula, repeated on many stelae, is: 'an offering given by the king, an offering given by Anubis, a thousand loaves, a thousand jugs of beer, a thousand oxen, a thousand geese for the vital power of life for whomsoever'.

The *ritual of the opening of the mouth*[43] is more explicit:

'O, undead', proclaims the magician,
'I give you a thousand loaves,
I give you a thousand jugs of beer,
I give you a thousand bulls,
I give you a thousand birds,
I give you a thousand pieces of linen,
I give you a thousand garments,
I give you a thousand gazelles,
I give you a thousand antelopes,
I give you a thousand bovidae (oxen),
I give you a thousand heads of small livestock,
I give you a thousand geese,

I give you a thousand heads of wildfowl,
I give you a thousand cranes,
I give you a thousand pigeons,
I give you a thousand pieces of meat cut up in the abattoir,
I give you a thousand loaves baked in the courtyard,
I give you a thousand grains of incense,
I give you a thousand pots of oil,
I give you a thousand ewers of fresh water,
I give you a thousand divine offerings,
I give you a thousand choice morsels from the offering table,
I give you a thousand pieces of choice meat,
I give you a thousand offering bouquets,
I give you a thousand foods,
I give you a thousand good and pure things, a thousand of
everything which is excellent, delicious and twice pure, des-
tined for your *ka*, whosoever!'

To this appetising list we should add honey, an extraordinary
food which travels in a divine ship to elude the grasshoppers.
The hearts of the gods are bitter until they receive honey—they
recover their well-being by eating it. It will always be so for just
men.[44]

The goddess *Weret-hekau*, 'Great-in-magic', is mistress of
nourishment. She takes the form of the double uraeus on the
king's brow. Eating and drinking are not secular acts. They are
the most immediate expressions of an alchemy which works
inside the body. In some circumstances, too, it is necessary to
take magical precautions. Thus, a spell must be recited while
drinking beer. Seth is summoned, the god of the power of life
and the heart, the centre of spiritual equilibrium.[45] Beer is seen
as a drink which brings health, or even healing. It acts as a purge
for the stomach. But there is a risk of drunkenness; a man who
drinks it is compared to Seth the drunkard. The use of beer in
magic drives away demonic influences. When the spell is recited
and the beer drunk, it is advisable to spit some out. In so doing
the demon that is in the stomach is addressed and named. It is
called 'death'. Its father is also named, 'he who causes heads to

fall'. Thanks to this identification the sick man is healed of his ills.[46]

The magician also utters spells over other liquids such as water and wine: those who drink them enjoy supernatural powers which spread throughout their bodies.

The magician speaks to the guardian of the Great House and asks him to open the door, for he is Re and the Nile.[47] He states that the doors of the *Duat* are open to him, and that he leaves by the sacred portal. But a magic ritual is needed to pass through one of these innumerable gates. The spell must be recited over a drawing of seven sacred eyes. Then a mixture of beer and natron is drunk.

Beer, with bread, is the basic energy-giving food. Nevertheless, to quench the rather supernatural thirst of a godlike child, 'the great stream' is used, which flows from the sky, an analogy with the milk of the sacred cow that nourished the infant pharaoh. This is a magical nourishment for it confers exceptional vitality on its happy recipients.

One must not joke about the sacred foods and handle them carelessly. There are certain prohibitions which every qualified magician knows in detail. Eating 'taboo' foods makes one ill. Thus, as we recalled earlier, Horus himself suffered from a serious indisposition after eating a fish sacred both to Re and to the falcon, his own sacred animal. These pains required the ministrations of Isis. As for the magician, when he treats similar cases, he recites the spells over a new plate painted with yellow ochre. He smears honey over the man who suffers from the pains which the god endured. Once he is washed he will be cured.[48]

No detailed study has been made of food in pharaonic Egypt. We do know, however, that the ancient Egyptians relished the pleasures of the table whose magic, whether ritual or not, was not lost on them.

Magical Plants

The earth produces a magical protection which is used by the exorcist to combat evil. When a venomous creature's poison falls on the earth, it is destroyed. The earth, father of the gods, quenches the destructive fire.[49] The morning dew, sent by the sky to bathe the plants with a divine flow, was reputed to cure paralysed limbs.

'When the gods' plants are on your head,' proclaims a ritual, 'all of life's protections you receive . . . The plants that rise from the earth come to you, the original flax of the Field of Reeds, the original regenerative plants of the field of joy, the odour of choice things which clothes the gods when they set forth. It comes to you like a precious shroud, it preserves you like a wrapping, it makes you grow like a piece of linen, it knits your bones like an immaculate bandage.[50]

All the essential plants of Egypt, papyrus, flax, and the precious substances, myrrh, incense and honey, are of divine origin. They are, in reality, the tears of Horus, the blood of Geb, the tears of Shu, of Tefnut, and those of Re which fell from the sky to earth.[51] Certain plants play a special role: for example, acacia, the symbol of regeneration, or juniper, which is said to give light.

To care for breasts, the divine models for which are those of Isis which fed the heavenly twins, Shu and Tefnut, many herbs are used, particularly reeds.[52] Even the effect of venom is reversed by the application of lotus to the wound.[53] As for mandragora root, it can make a man sleep for two days.[54] Garlic is used in the house to close the mouths of male and female serpents and of scorpions. They are the arms of Re, Horus, Thoth, of the Great and Lesser Ennead which, alerted by the use of garlic, will kill a sick man's enemies. The spell must be recited over garlic which has been ground into a powder and mixed with beer. This is none other than the 'white Eye of Horus'. The house is permeated with it during the night so that no dangerous creature will enter it.[55] The onion also proves efficacious. As for *'ash* pine (cedar), it bears a fluid which heightens the magician's perceptions.

Vegetable matter is widely used in magic; so too is wax, a

basic ingredient in the manufacture of magic figurines, which are covered with inscriptions and thrown in the fire, as a sign of the destruction of the enemy they represent. Magicians were particularly expert in the art of making ointments. They had the use of magnificent laboratories in the temples. One of their most marvellous products was 'the great secret ointment of the House of Life' which serves to protect the buildings in the same way as it maintains the parts of the human body in harmony.

Knowledge of perfumes if indispensable in the other world. The justified dead replaces the stink of putrefaction with that of myrrh which Hathor herself places on his head, his smell will be that of the incense which the goddess uses, his scent is a precious oil with which Hathor anoints herself.[56]

Who can doubt that the world of plants is shot through with magic vibrations? Can there be a more peaceful moment than when one breathes the fresh air beneath the leaves of the ancient persea tree of Heliopolis, or awakes each morning in a garden gazing on the sun's rays, after one has passed the tests of initiation and the soul is raised towards the light?

9 Magical Love

When men go out hunting serpents and scorpions, the women stay at home. Since my host in Luxor had done me the great honour of presenting me to his wife, I ventured, with great care, to question him about the role of women in magic. He reflected for a long time before replying. 'Love between a man and a woman,' he stated, 'is not what many people believe. Love is a gift of magic. My wife and I have the same experience of life.'

So many texts, so much sculpture showing couples tenderly entwined, so many evocations of human love as a symbol of divine love ... yes, ancient Egypt celebrated magical love in many different forms.

Spells

In a charm intended to inspire love, the magician greets the Seven Hathors, Re-Horakhte, the father of the gods and the masters of the heaven and the earth. He demands this of them—that the woman he loves will seek him as a cow seeks grass, a mother her child, or the shepherd his flock. If these powers should refuse to help, the magician would put Busiris to the torch and burn Osiris.[1]

This shows that love—such a magical energy—demands the frequent attentions of specialists who are aware of the soul's passions as well as those of the body. Spell 576 of the *Coffin Texts* is dedicated to the divine power that dwells in the phallus of the man those thoughts are both in heaven and on earth. The man who knows the magic spell will copulate in this world by night and day, and desire will enter the woman to whom he makes love.

A Greek papyrus in the Bibliothèque Nationale in Paris records texts which were intended to inspire love in a woman, and recalls the legend of Isis who, at the height of summer, goes to the mountains, wandering and unhappy. Thoth is troubled, seeing her in that state. Why is Isis' face covered with dust, why are her eyes full of tears? The reason is simple and tragic. She has found her sister Nephthys sleeping with Osiris, her husband. Then comes a terrible curse which will terrify her rival and cast a spell on the various parts of her body.[2] Late Greco-Egyptian magic often loses itself in these byways. One Greek papyrus[3] has no hesitation in appealing to Anubis, who officiates at the funerary rites, to awaken love in a woman: 'Anubis, god of the earth, underworld and heavens, dog, dog, dog, use all your strength and all your power on Titer, who was borne by Sophia (Wisdom). Strip from her her pride, prudence and modesty, and bring her to me here, at my feet, languid with passion, at every hour of the day or night, dreaming of me ceaselessly, when she eats and when she drinks, when she works and even when she makes love, when she rests, when she dreams and when she is dreaming; when, tormented by you, she hastens, languishing for me, wholeheartedly, her soul filled with generosity, offering herself to me, and fulfils the duty of women towards men, serving to satisfy my lust and her own, never bored, without shame, rubbing her thigh against mine, belly to belly, her black down against my black down in the sweetest way! Yes, my master, bring me Titer, to whom Sophia gave birth, bring me Hermes to whom Hermione gave birth.'

The magical techniques for making a woman fall in love are often extremely complicated. One must use various vegetable products, grind them, put them in a jar, add oil at a precise moment, be ruled by the phases of the moon, recite the spells, rise early to go into a garden, and there pick a vine shoot in the left hand, then, when it has grown seven fingers in length, carry it home in the right hand, extract the oil from a fish which has been chopped up, tie its tail, etc.[4] There is nothing simple in this maze of practices.

The so-called technique of the scarab beetle and cup of wine is scarcely more practicable. To make a woman fall in love, it is recommended that one should take a small scarab beetle without horns. This must be done at sunrise. The beetle is drowned in the milk from a black cow, and left there until the evening. Then it must be taken out again, its underparts covered with sand, and covered with a round piece of material. Incense must be burnt before it. The day after, it is dry. Divide it in the middle with a bronze knife. Cook it with woodvine, mash it with apple pips mixed with the magician's urine or sweat. With this make a ball which is put into wine and then make the woman one desires drink it.[5]

The good old magic potions, it's plain to see, were given free rein in popular magic. But they required ingredients which were almost impossible to obtain, such as hairs from the head of a man who had died a violent death or seven grains of spelt taken from a tomb. Tricks like pouring rose-scented ointment into a lamp or pulping the fruit of the acacia tree mixed with honey to get a substance with which to anoint the phallus, are quicker. The results, however, are not guaranteed. A woman's love is such a complex emotion that this type of magic yields poor results most of the time.

The only true magic of love is in the identification of the magician with Osiris with whom Isis was so besotted that she raised him from the dead. That magic is an integral part of the initiation into the greater mysteries and of the transmutation of human love into divine energy.

Magic and Childbirth

Birth is a time of as much danger as happiness for mother and child, whose life is threatened by evil spirits. The magician must help the woman in labour by obtaining the help of good spirits armed with knives who have at their disposal weapons as powerful as those of their dreadful enemies. It is also advisable to appeal to the great gods. During a difficult birth it is sometimes the mother and sometimes the child who needs the magician's care. He invokes a goddess and a Horus. But these are busy taking measurements in the fields and keep him waiting. Free at last, they appear before the child as examples of the just who tend their plots of land in the heavenly regions. Earthly birth is then a prelude to heavenly birth. The surveyor's cord is likened to the umbilical cord.[6]

Charms to speed up birth are very rare. As Hathor and Isis found themselves in the most delicate of situations, so women who suffer similar pain are helped by the greatest gods who come to their aid.* It is helpful to carry protective amulets, especially those of the joyous dwarf, Bes. The woman in labour can also appeal directly to Hathor for help.[8]

Gynaecologists must be magicians. Dealing with a prolapsed uterus, for instance, is not simply a mechanical operation. Surgery and magic must join forces to make a statuette of an ibis in wax, and burn it in the fire. The smoke will enter the woman's genitals, and with Thoth's help everything will be restored to its proper place.

One goddess is particularly concerned in the business of childbirth. The goddess Meskhenet, descendant of Atum, daughter of Shu and Tefnut, fulfils her duty by making the spirit enter the body of the child who has just left its mother's womb. She gives him the heavenly and earthly powers he needs, prevents him being cursed and drives all evil away from him. The magician utters the spells over two bricks where the birthing woman lies. He throws incense and bird grease in the fire. Thus all will go well.[9]

To speed Isis' delivery, the magician appeals to Re and Atum, the gods of the Western region, the divine assembly which judges the entire earth, and the council of gods of Heliolopolis and those of Letopolis. Isis is in pain. Her pregnancy has reached its term. If Horus is not born, what sorrows there will be. No more heaven, no more earth, no more offerings for the gods, universal troubles![10]

---

* There are various spells to make birth easier. Here is one: 'Open me! I am he who gives a great offering, the builder of a pylon for Hathor, mistress of Dendera, who rises so that she may give birth,' meaning Hathor.[7]

Isis is the supreme mother. If her labour were difficult the consequences would be terrifying. The very principle of life would be at risk. That is why every mother-to-be puts her trust in her, while at the same time asking the hippopotamus goddess Thoueris (Tauert) for help, 'the great', pregnant female, holding the hieroglyph of protection. Two figurines of Thoueris, in the Berlin Museum, have slits in which one can put pieces of the pregnant woman's clothes. Another figurine was filled with milk. The liquid flowed gently from the hippopotamus-goddess's breast, guaranteeing that the mother would have no trouble in feeding her infant. There was a group of twelve hippopotamus-goddesses, each being responsible for one month of the year. In the beginning the hippopotamus-goddess Ipet was identified with the sky. Later, she presided over mammisis—special sanctuaries sacred to the rites of birth. Fat Thoueris, with her enormous belly and the paws and muzzle of a lion, is not ugly to look at; beneath that amazing shape she hides her true nature which is revealed to us by an inscription on a statue:[11] 'I am Thoueris, in all her power, she who fights anything which might harm you and drives away those who might do violence to your son, Horus. I am Ipet who dwells in the horizon and whose knife protects the universal Master, the mistress who is feared, she of the ornate appearance who beheads those who rebel against her.'

When the time comes for birth, Nut, the sky goddess, is invoked. In her are all the gods, the stars who transmit light and are the souls of the glorified. The magician asks the vault of the stars to descend on the woman in labour and protect her. A more concrete personification of the sky goddess is the sow Reret, who protects humans from poisonous bites and also blesses the childbed. This sow, feeding her large litter, was worshipped until the end of the Middle Ages in the West where she appeared among the carvings in the cathedrals.

The Child

A child is a delicate creature, above all when it is newborn. That is why the magician uses a great many spells to protect it. At Heliopolis, on the first and last days of the lunar month, there are festivals to safeguard mother and child.

The infant is protected just like the sky, earth, the day and the night, and the gods who laid the foundations of the earth. The gods protect the child's name, the milk he sucks, the clothes he wears, the age in which he lives, the amulets made for him and placed around his neck.[12] Spells are recited over the child at first light. The hand and seal of the sun-god are the mother's protection.* Each morning and evening she recites the magic spells over an amulet which hangs round her child's neck. She prays to the rising sun. She implores him to take away the dead who would like to steal her child. 'It is Re, my lord, who saves me,' she affirms; nor does she give her child to the thief from the kingdom of the dead.[13]

In opposition to the Egyptian magician there are often mages from other lands. The mother protects her child against foreign magic by encircling him in her arms. She particularly distrusts Nubian or Asiatic sorcery. Whether they are slaves or nobility, she casts a terrible curse upon them: Let them become as Vomit or Urine![14]

The baby must be watched over at all times: is he warm enough in his nest, for he is compared to a nestling? Does his mother take good care of him? Is she there? If not, is the nurse? Is anyone watching his breathing? To avoid any trouble, knots are made and spells uttered over little golden and garnet balls and over a seal showing a crocodile and a hand.[15]

If the child develops a suspicious swelling, he is reminded that he is Horus and the demon which appears as an aggressor with

---

* Still, in some circumstances magic is needed to attract the sun's influence. To do this, choose a pure young boy, recite the written spell over him, place him facing east, and give him a new brick to hold as the sun rises. Then, place a piece of linen behind the boy who has his eyes closed. Tap him on the head with a finger of the right hand (*Leyden Magical Papyrus*, 165–7).

his sharp knife like a butcher is driven off. The swelling goes
down and the pus runs out. Faced with this rather disgusting
sight, the magician conjures up a delightful scene in which he
lies with marvellous women with hair perfumed with myrrh.[16]

The *Metternich Stela* explains that Horus was bitten in a field
at Heliopolis while Isis was occupied in the upper rooms, making
libations in honour of her brother Osiris. Horus cried out in pain.[17]
Isis appealed to the heavenly powers for help. To heal Horus,
the nurses of the holy city of Buto watch over him, following
his progress through the world of men to the point where he
takes possession of the throne of the Two Lands. His mother's
magical power is his protection, she surrounds him with love and
makes men go in fear of him.[18]

This basic myth of Isis and Horus, the Mother and Child,
haunts Egyptian thought. The fragility of human existence and
the power of magic confront each other here. The drama which
is Isis' life is poignant. Escaping from Seth's fury, she hides her
child and goes off to find food. When she returns she finds Horus
unconscious. She makes enquiries of the inhabitants of the marsh.
Horus has been bitten by a scorpion or serpent. Isis clasps Horus
in her arms and chants the litany, 'Horus has been bitten.' On
the advice of the scorpion goddess Serket, she calls on the barque
of the sun, which is forced to stop. Thoth descends from it. He
orders the poison to disappear, so that the cosmic disturbances
caused by the immobilisation of the solar vessel may cease.[19]

There is no learning but magic. How, without magic, may the
watchful mother ward off evil spirits? To cure the fever in a
child's stomach, Isis and Nephthys send an appeal to Geb, father
of the gods. They recite the spell over two images of Thoth,
drawn on a man's hand in fresh ink.[20]

To help the child grow, he is made to eat a morsel of his
placenta, mashed in milk. If he vomits, he will die. If he swallows
it easily, he will have a long life. The royal placenta was actually
looked upon as one of the symbols of the principle of life. All
the time, we must glorify the latter against the lurking powers
of death. The demon of illness comes out of the shadows. It has
its nose at the back, its face turned round. The demon must be

prevented from clasping the child, approaching him or taking him, in other words, making him die. The mother is always worried about her child's health. At any time, a disturbing shape, a female phantom, could get into the house. The mother asks it: 'Have you come to embrace this child? I will not allow it? Have you come to carry him off? I will not permit it.' The spectre is a dead woman. Thrown by the mother's questions, she no longer knows why she came. She flees and loses touch with the newborn.[21]

The ancient Egyptians had an acute feeling for a medical magic in which the environment played a great part. The negative forces are not only driven from the child's body but also from the house. No one can be healthy in unhealthy surroundings. Happily the mother has one wonderful remedy: her milk. The milk of the goddesses revives the pharaoh, that of the mother chases the demons away from children. This extra-ordinary food cures colics, colds and burns and bestows energy and power. Milk which has been 'charged' magically by spells is poured into a jar in the form of a mother holding a child in her lap. The milk of the mother or nurse is thought of as a 'protective water' which shelters the newborn from illness. Did not Isis, on leaving the weaving room, put out the fire which hurt Horus with her milk?[22]

Human milk and grains of perfumes are excellent aids in fighting one painful affliction, a cold in the head. 'Stop streaming, head cold, son of the head cold, which affects the seven orifices of the head,' says the magician; Re's servants address their prayers to Thoth and the magician brings the remedy, namely the milk of a woman who has given birth to a son and some grains of well chosen perfume. In this way Thoth cured Re of sinusitis by which he was badly affected.[23]

The state of childhood must be regained. The pharaoh becomes a child again to drink at the source of life. It is the same for the initiate who enters into the kingdom of the Underworld, as the ritual proclaims: 'You are going to begin to walk again, as a little child, because of what has been done for your *ka* according to the decree of the Sovereign of the four pillars of the sky, giving you a perfect, careful and complete funeral.'[24]

This is the beautiful purpose of magical love: to raise from a child a man whose spirit opens itself to the knowledge of the divine, a being whose sensitive intelligence captures the pervasive energies of the universe.

10 The Animal World

My hosts in Luxor loved animals, even scorpions and snakes. In their home, dogs and cats had agreed a truce. But the patriarch and his family treated them neither with indifference nor with pity. 'Those creatures,' the Old Man confided to me, 'have souls. They have no need to know the spirits for they are spirits.' Of course, I asked a thousand questions about the Egyptian gods with their animal heads, about the sacred animals and about the ancient Egyptian's extraordinary love of the animal world in which the divine shows itself so powerfully and distinctly. Much of the time he was content to nod his head, as if time had been abolished, as if the spiritual landscape of ancient Egypt was still laid out before our eyes.

The Falcon, the Cat and Company

The falcon, the incarnation of Horus and protector of royalty, is naturally one of the most important magical animals. Chapter 134 of the *Book of the Dead* puts it this way: 'Words to be spoken over a standing falcon with the white crown on his head, and over Atum, Shu, Tefnut, Geb, Nut, Osiris, Isis, Seth, Nephthys, painted in white on a new cup and placed in the above ship with the image of the fortunate one whom you wish to glorify, anointed with rouge; burning incense is presented to them.'

The spells of the *Coffin Texts*[1] give the magician the power to become a falcon. The gods are terrified. He is fierce and swift. He roams the paths of eternity. He becomes the man-falcon who is able to return to earth to take vengeance on his enemies by

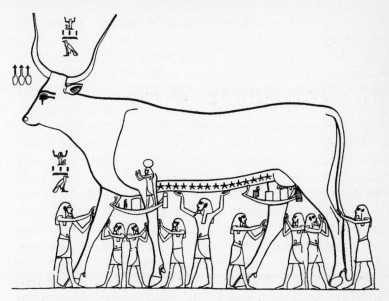

The heavenly Cow, the foster-mother, supported by genies. The divine barques circulate within her. From her comes the regenerating milk upon which the king and the universe feed.

tearing them with his talons, destroying their family and home. The Eye of Horus is his guide, Horus' magic powers are his power, no one can withstand him. It is in the form of a falcon that the magician comes and goes to the very ends of the sky, to receive the words of Geb, the god of the earth, and to ask him for the Word which can be used by the Master of everything.[2] As a golden falcon, the magician seizes whatever he finds in the empty spaces of the sky and feeds in Horus' slaughterhouses.[3] Thus it is by becoming one with the heavenly power of the falcon that the magician acquires Horus' power.

The cat, an animal much loved by the Egyptians, is not only a guileful and intelligent feline. It is also the incarnation of Re, Hathor and Bastet. The magician appeals to Re because a scorpion has stung a cat on a remote path. She howled with pain. Her cries went up to heaven. 'Come to your daughter!' the magician pleads. 'The venom has entered her body, and is spreading through her flesh.' Re arrives. 'Have no fear, my daughter,' he says to comfort her. The god stands behind her with the sign of life. Each part of the cat's body is identified with parts of the bodies of the gods.* Her being becomes the symbol of all the divine forces. That is why she must be cured, and that is accomplished. 'It is Re who recited that,' concludes the magical text. Thus the incantation was recited by the Light in person.[4]

Another cat, perhaps the civet cat, is the symbolic animal of the goddess Mafdet. Swift and agile, she works against the magician's enemies who seek to destroy his sexual potency and his creative faculties. The words are to be spoken over the phallus of a donkey, whose shape has been given to a cake, given the name of his enemy and those of his father and mother. It is placed on a piece of meat and given to a cat who will dispose of the evil by eating it.[5]

The dog also deserves proper consideration. To gain its loyalty, according to a Coptic papyrus, the magician employs extraordinary means. He ties together the sky, the earth, the four pillars of the earth, the sun to the east, the moon to the west (preventing them from rising), and the fields to the earth (preventing them from producing). Each bond is knotted in such a manner that it cannot be untied. But the dog is not always docile. He can rebel and bite. That is why there is a magic spell against a dog's bite. The magician states that his mouth is filled with the blood of a black dog. He summons his attacker, who is one of the ten animals who belong to Anubis, to extract his 'venom'. Otherwise he will let it loose upon him.[6]

In the desert of Ancient Egypt lions were hunted. Wild animals, it was said, keep their eyes open while sleeping. Pharaoh is

---

* Her head is Re's, her eyes are those of the divine Master who brings light to the Two Lands; her nose is Thoth's; her ears, those of the Master of the universe who hears the voice of any who ask for justice, wherever he may be; her mouth, Atum's; her breast, Thoth's, who gives the air which the throat needs to breathe; her heart is that of Ptah, who frees the body for all poisons, her paws are the hands of the Great and the Lesser Ennead; Her stomach is that of Osiris; her thighs, Montu's; her calves, Khonsu's; her haunches those of Horus; the soles of her feet, Re's.

identified with the lion, for he is all vigilance, all power, casting a shining light which protects him from dangerous beings. Spell 83 of the *Coffin Texts* is to be recited over the forequarters of a lion. The amulet is fastened to the neck of the magician who is going down into the necropolis. It enables him to exercise his mastery of the winds of heaven and become their king. The man who knows the good spell 'will not die anew'. His enemies will have no power over him. No contrary magic will nail him to the earth. He will leave the necropolis as he likes and become a creature of light in the company of Osiris.

A common animal of the countryside of Ancient Egypt was the hippopotamus who is an ambivalent creature, sometimes benefi-cent, sometimes maleficent. One myth tells of the victory of Horus the harpooner over Seth the hippopotamus, which symbolises the triumph of light over darkness and all the forces of evil. The 'festival of harpooning the hippopotamus' was known from the time of the 1st Dynasty, the pachyderm being identified with the king's enemies. The points of the harpoons were likened to the rays of the sun in the *Pyramid Texts*. The magician, in the *Coffin Texts*, is a harpooner standing in his ship. He kills the monster, thus taking on the stature of crowned Horus.

The hippopotamus is evil when it appears swollen, a heavy and powerful monster who crushes the vegetation and pillages the population. As Pharaoh was the first harpooner, his actions must be repeated. But the female hippopotamus is seen as a kindly crea-ture. At Thebes she is a white goddess who destroys the king's enemies, as she did at the beginning of the world; she is not har-pooned, but celebrated as a symbol of maternal fecundity.[7]

The Scarab

The *Ebers Papyrus*[8] advises one to eat this—odd advice which is more understandable when one knows that the Egyptian name for a scarab is *kheper*, a word which also means 'to grow, to become, to change oneself'. A powerful talisman, the scarab of green stone is placed over the heart of a man who has been purified with myrrh, following the rite of the opening of the mouth (thus of resurrection).

The scarab beetle is one of the most surprising of creatures. It rolls before it its eggs which have been deposited in faeces and shaped into a sphere, which it pushes along with its back feet. Thus it imitates the course of the sun.

To summon the gods, the magician takes a scarab and drowns it in the white milk of a black cow. Then he puts it on a brazier. The magic will go into action at the desired moment and the light will come.[9] The 'scarabs' were also a sort of seal, mostly used to stamp official documents. Worn as amulets, they proved to have remarkable powers, giving their owners the assurance of a happy future and an ever-growing spiritual life.

The three most dangerous animals—because they possess considerable power—are the crocodile, the scorpion and the snake.

The *crocodile* is particularly formidable for it could rob a dead man of his magic powers. There are spells to use to drive it away: 'Get back, be gone! Do not come against me! I live through my magic power! Let your face turn towards Maat (meaning, the harmony of the world which will appease the crocodile).' The magician converses with the monster who speaks to him of the sky whose virtues he knows and holds in his mouth. The magician must avoid a dramatic fight between celestial magic and earthly magic. He must master the crocodile, take his power from him, not destroy him.

At each of the cardinal points which mark the limits of the cosmos there sits a crocodile. That of the West eats the stars. That of the East lives on the beings who eat their own filth. That of the South lives on excrement. That of the North eats the hours. The magician vanquishes all four and declares: 'I am clothed and armed with Re's magic power: he is on me, fully realised for me, amplified for me, enlarged for my throat.'

The 'earthly' crocodile is no less disturbing than the celestial crocodile, particularly to the cattle who cross a branch of the river and are in danger of being attacked. The monster personifies lurking, invisible, agonising death. That is why the herdsman, to preserve the lives of the beasts in his herd, must behave like a magician. He must be vigilant and blind the crocodile. Thus, the attacker will not be able to see his intended victims and will not approach.[11] The herdsman-magician pronounces a curse that will stop the crocodile seizing anything with his claws, or opening his mouth. The water will become a flame that will consume him. A special charm robs the crocodile of the use of his tail. Sixty-seven gods will dig their fingers into his eyes while he is tied to the mooring post of Osiris or to the four green stone posts which are in the prow of Re's ship.

The magician takes the identity of Amon. He recites the words over an image of this same god Amon, with four faces on one neck, drawn on the earth, a crocodile beneath his feet, eight gods on his right and his left.[12] According to the *Harris Magical Papyrus*, the sailor who takes on the role of the magician stands at the prow of a boat holding a clay egg in his hand. In this way he resembles the sun rising over the waters in an egg and dispersing the darkness. The malevolent inhabitants of the waters are afraid when they see this sight and dive back into their refuges. The boat continues on its way in total safety. If the crocodile should nevertheless shoot out of the water menacingly, the sailor will throw the egg into the water and put the demon to flight.[13]

Some stelae show Horus standing with his feet on the head of two crocodiles. The child-god is naked. These objects are of various sizes, some reaching a metre in height, and others being no bigger than an amulet. These stelae were placed in temples as often as in houses. The donor had himself portrayed holding this precious stela.

Statue and stela are placed on a plinth in which two basins are carved, at different levels, joined by a channel. When water is poured over the monument, it impregnates the texts and the magical drawings. Anyone who drinks the water will be protected from evil.*

* An example of a text (Statue, Louvre, E 10 777) is: 'The man who drinks this water ensures that his own heart, his very breast, will be strengthened thanks to the magical protection which he has acquired. Venom will not enter his heart, nor burn in his breast, for his name is Horus, for Osiris is his father's name, for Neith is his mother's name.'

It is interesting that spell 991 of the *Coffin Texts* allows the magician to become Sobek, that is the divine crocodile! 'I am the master of the power and strength which has taken the form of a crocodile,' he affirms. Lord of the Nile, he is also called 'fair of face' and 'great seducer' who ravishes all the women. There is also a way to lay a quick spell upon a vase so that the gods will enter it and reply truthfully to the magician; all that is needed is to burn a crocodile egg-shell.[14]

The *scorpion*, the brother of the snake, is frightening. He sits at the crossroads, waiting for the traveller by night. As for the latter, may his heel be bronze and the ball of his foot be ivory! Thanks to magic, the walker's feet are the seven falcons which stand at the prow of Re's ship:[15] what better protection against being stung? However, even the gods have fallen victim to the scorpion although they did not die. A man who has been stung by a scorpion takes on their identity to be able to use their skill in fighting evil. He must know the myths, such as the one about Re's daughter, the cat who was stung by a scorpion, then healed by Re.

The magician who created the healing statue of Djed-her called 'the saviour' speaks in these terms: 'I have put the inscriptions on this statue in accordance with what is written in Re's holy books, in the words which describe the whole technique of subduing-the-scorpion, to bring back to life, by this process, all people and all animals and protect them against the venom of all snakes both male and female, all reptiles, by doing that which is pleasing to the heart of the Lord of the gods.'[16] As Horus-the-Justified, the magician subdues the scorpion. His father's protector, he has placed his arms behind Re. His abilities as hypnotist assure him life, prosperity and health. He takes care of all his limbs, calming sorrows, driving away evil. Re rises again healed, more beautiful than before. It will be thus with every sick man who is cared for by a good magician.[17]

He orders the scorpion to keep calm. He shuts its mouth. If it moves he will cut off the seventy-seven heads from the neck of the great god, the hand of Horus will blind the eye of Seth, will seize the mouth of the Great Ennead, will burn Osiris. Let the scorpion stay still as Seth before Ptah![18]

'I am Osiris,' the magician declares, to impress the scorpion. At the same time he shows himself as the serpent of Heliopolis, who can fight any evil being.

The scorpion, which was used to write the name of one of the first pharaohs, is not a wholly negative influence. It holds the spirit of a goddess, Serket, who reigns over a brotherhood of warriors to whom she told the secrets of the scorpion's power. The water scorpion, though, is inoffensive. That is the one drawn in hieroglyphs, for they, being living images, cannot allow dangerous creatures amongst them.

There is an Isis-scorpion which protects Horus and the king.[19] 'Lady of light who illumines the Two Lands, she is likened to the star Sothis.' It is said that she emits a radiance to chase away the darkness. The scorpion-goddess is known from the earliest times, but the first representations of it appear in the Nubian temples of the 18th Dynasty. She is Isis the Great, to whom this prayer is addressed: 'Come to me, Great Isis, deign to guarantee my protection, save me from the reptiles and let their jaws be sealed, let their noses be blocked.' The goddess grants her devotees 'life, health, a long life and a long and perfect old age'. Isis-scorpion tramples on snakes and crocodiles. A text in the temple at Edfu defines her as the daughter if Re, who destroys the enemies of the sun and the opponents of Horus, as 'the imposing scorpion, venerable reptile whose venom strikes like lightning, piercing in a flash the soil of enemies, so that they die immediately when it strikes.'

This is the paradox of magic: Isis, the sworn enemy of scorpions, is also their goddess, venerated in the town of Coptos. When she seeks to escape from Seth, Thoth advises her to hide with her child Horus, so that he will grow and rejoin the gods who will place him on the throne of his father to reign over the Two Lands. Isis sets out in the evening. For her protection against a possible attack by Seth, she is accompanied by a strange band— seven scorpions! She orders them to treat both rich and poor in the same way, to be stern but fair with the human race. When she enters a woman's home, the woman, frightened by the scorpions, shuts the door. They are furious and confer together. They give all their venom to one of their number who manages to gain entry to the house and sting the son of the bad hostess. But Isis will not assent to the death of such an innocent. She creates magic spells to save the child and drives out the poison after addressing the seven scorpions by name. The words she spoke serve as remedies to heal any child who is stung by a scorpion: 'Let the child live,' she says, 'and the poison perish as Re lives when the poison perishes! As Horus is healthy for his mother Isis' sake, thus is the sick one healthy!'[20]

The magician knows how to use the scorpion to fight against a snake, so that it stings and destroys the snake. He can also become the scorpion as is proved by a strange symbolic detail: the magician's plait is that of the scorpion goddess and, more precisely, the tail of an animal. It is therefore possible for him to slip into the fearful scorpion and direct it as he pleases, if he is a master of the magic art.

The *Pyramid Texts* attach great importance to magical texts which are intended to nullify the danger presented by the *snake*. They are written in strange and incomprehensible words, collections of sounds which are considered most effective when spoken aloud. Entire papyri are devoted to charms against snakes.[21] 'His face falls on his face' is the classic formula to express the destruction of the snake; reptiles are ordered not to attack the pharaoh for he represents the gods on earth. Re curses the serpent, Isis binds it, Nephthys enchains it.[22] The magician sends a special appeal to Re, to prevent the venom of any serpent in the universe from taking effect. The luminous power of the sun god bestows a special gift upon the magician.[23]

To protect oneself against snakes, it is best to stand facing the East and to acknowledge Amun's sovereignty, wearing the white crown. Keep silent, meditate and gather power. No longer will one fear meeting the serpent described as 'black of face, blind in both eyes, with a white eye, which writhes as it moves.' The reptile is identified as Seth, who came from the thighs of Isis.

The fire caused by the serpent's bite is compared to that dangerous flame which Horus the magician, master of fire, must master.

The serpent is 'he of the fire', the being to conquer. The magician, become like the sun, leaves the Island of the Flames unharmed, for he is able to smother the harmful effects of the fire when it flares up.[24]

According to the *Pyramid Texts* the snakes are coiled one around the other. The magician asks the earth to swallow them, and orders the monsters to lie down and creep; their heads are cut off, their poison fangs are empty. The magician also makes the male snake bite the female and vice versa. If he acts correctly, he will enjoy the protection of the sky and the earth, both equally necessary, to reinforce the effectiveness of the spells that seal the mouths of the reptiles who dwell in the sky, earth, and water.[25]

The *Metternich Stela* calls upon the serpent as the one who is both in the hole and at the opening of the hole, and also as the one who is on the road. In other words, a constant peril which one would avoid. How can one travel without fear? By taking the identity of the bull Mnevis, Sepa of the thousand feet, the scorpion–goddess Serket or more important divinities such as Thoth or Re. Awed, the snake will not bite the traveller invested with these divine personalities.[26] To be sure, one must not forget to use an appropriate spell: 'O every male or female snake, every scorpion, every reptile! May your mouths be sealed! It is Re who has stopped up your throats. It is Sekhmet who has cut off your tongues. It is Thoth who has blinded your eyes. It is Heka, the fourth of the great gods, who is Osiris' protection. These are they who protect the sick, and all men and all animals who suffer this day.'[27]

A serious problem is that some snakes are themselves magicians. To drive away one of these raging reptiles when it attacks, one must scatter the books of magic which it uses, by means of Isis' clay, which comes from the armpit of the scorpion goddess. The magician's finger is his guardian, the clay blocks up the serpent's hole.[28] Geb, the earth-god, is father of the serpents over which he has power. He is often regarded as the creator of Atum. Father and prince of the gods, he is the head of an Ennead. The Greeks made him their Chronos, who became the Saturn of the Romans.[29] Chapter 163 of the *Book of the Dead* recommends

pronouncing the magic words over a snake who has two legs and
wears the solar disc between his horns; at his side are two sacred
eyes with two legs and two wings. This image is drawn with
dried myrrh mixed with pomegranate juice on a strip of green
material, which is wrapped round the body of a man to give him
magical protection.

The *serpent* is often considered to be beneficial. Thus Aha, a
good spirit serpent, was put at the entrance to the temples. It
guards the threshold.[30] Another snake protects the royal palace or
encircles the table of offerings, sheltering it from evil influences.[31]

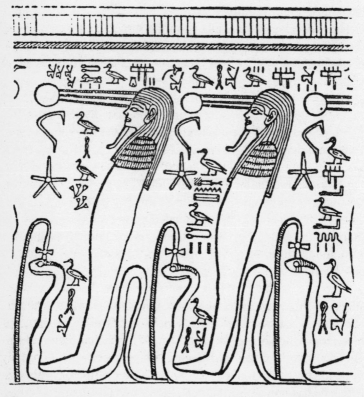

*Phases of the mutation of the energy of creation: The rays of light penetrate
the heads of mummified beings who serve as channels for the light which is
then transferred to the powers of earth symbolised by serpents. A curved
pillar of fire enters their eyes.*

Renenutet, a woman with the head of a snake, watches over the harvests and reaping. Above all she is the foster-mother snake who takes care of life on earth. According to spell 85-8 of the *Coffin Texts*, death is the serpent-*nau*, bull of the Enneads, but it is not subject to any magic. Nothing harmful can touch it. Neither fire nor water can bring it harm. It will be as Re every day. Transformed into a serpent 'son-of-the-earth',[32] every night the magician is brought to earth renewed, rejuvenated.

Venom and *poison* are dreadful, for they enter into the veins of the body, disturbing the vital fluid and causing certain death. However, the magician's initiation enables him to familiarise himself with these dangers. He may even have been stung in a controlled fashion to test the actual effects of the poison. Djed-her the magician puts it in these terms: 'I drew near because I was bitten and fell ill. Then the venom left me. Let it be burnt, the venom which was in the body of this suffering man!'[33]

The suffering man is called 'lord of the night', meaning the time during which the invisible serpent is most dangerous. He is master of dark powers, he descended into the shadows and left them again.[34] The magician has lived through an initiation which is indispensable to one who wishes to fight this evil with any chance of success.

Poison is a force. As such a spell must be put on it. By blinding it with spells the magician prevents it circulating as it wishes. The venom has a face which it cannot raise, a head which will be turned backwards, it will wander without being able to reach its goal. It will not cry out with joy.

When the poison is ordered to fall to earth, leaving the sick man's body, a very special magical climate is created. There is the sound of wind, but no wind. There is the noise of water, but the flood has not come. One must be ready for the appearance of the sun's light, for the brilliance of the disk which will eventually vanquish the darkness. The magician looks at the sky and sees Re. It is he who will save him. 'O Re,' calls the magician, 'come, be a saviour now that I have seen you!' The poison will not work. He threatens the venom, and explains that its action could have catastrophic consequences on the order of the universe. 'If the venom works its way towards the heart of this man suffering here, it works its way towards Re's heart. If it seizes upon this man's heart, it seizes the hearts of the Souls of Heliopolis.'[36] The last catastrophe is impossible. As long as the magician does not suffer from the poison, Re will not go away, Thoth will not go away, Horus will not go away, the light will come, the rites will be performed in the temples.[37]

The exorcist's voice is strong when he challenges the poison, like the voice of Re when he speaks to his Ennead, like that of Thoth to his writings, as the flour to the grain, as Seth when he fights evil.[38] There is a spell which has stopped the poison from acting since 'the primordial time', when life came into existence. The words are spoken by Serket, the scorpion-goddess, calling on the god who created himself, formed the earth, the sky, the water, the breeze, life, the gods, men, the greater and lesser beasts, the reptiles, the birds and the fishes. Thus the magician is given the revelation that kingship over men and over gods is one and the same thing. It is by this mastery that he forces poison and venom to carry out his orders, speaking in a very hard voice: 'Leave, poison, come, scatter yourself on the earth! Horus curses you, he wipes you out, he grinds you underfoot. You do not rise, and you fall, you are feeble and do not struggle, you are blind and do not see, your head hangs and you do not lift up your face.'[39]

To combat the scorpion's dart, Isis uses an oil to which she says a special prayer. This true oil is compared to a raindrop, to a shower of Jupiter which falls from the sun's ship at dawn.[40] If anyone has drunk poison the magician remembers that he himself, Isis and Osiris have also drunk it and did not die from it. He will use 'Osiris' golden cup' which transforms any noxious liquid into a beneficial drink.[41] According to the *Metternich Stela* Isis and Nephthys spin and weave against the poison. Thus they create a cosmic network of harmonies which prevents the forces of evil from breaking out over the world. These two goddesses provide magicians with the bands and materials necessary for the practice of their art.

The magician, conqueror of the scorpion's dart, is seen as a king around whom the gods are assembled. If he has been

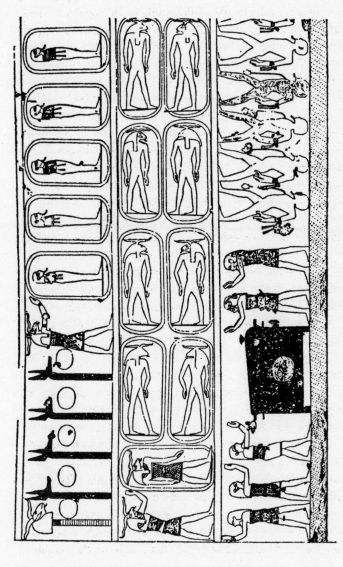

In the two upper registers a ram-genie, a form of the sun, generates the energy for growth, represented both as a man (upright) and as a ram-headed man (horizontal). In the bottom register, alongside bound people walking upside down, magicians cast spells over a mysterious chest from which emanates the energy of resurrection.

wounded in the battle, Isis comes to his aid, and advises him to lick the edges of the wound, for his tongue is that of the creator, Atum. Thus he will be instantly healed.[42]

Dozens of animals play a greater or lesser role in magic rituals. It would be pedantic to list them all here. Some surprising examples deserve a mention. For example, to drive away troublesome creatures which the magician has attracted unintentionally, he must put monkey droppings on a brazier. Ectoplasms and phantoms, annoyed by the spell, return to the dark places from which they came.[43]

The most modest creatures are not overlooked, for we know one spell to purify a fly[44] and stop it carrying dirt.

Spell 98 of the *Coffin Texts*, which concerns a heavenly journey of the magician's soul, must be recited over a head louse, placed on his knee until a fly swallows it.

But the major preoccupation of the magician who uses the powers of the animal world is to avoid falling beneath the claws of the most terrifying monster of all, 'the one who eats the West', crocodile-headed, with the hindquarters of the hippopotamus and a lion's mane. Her duty is to swallow and destroy any dead man who is found by the tribunal to be unjust. The magician must avoid such misfortune by his spells of knowledge, and clear this hurdle to reach the heavenly paradise.

Appendix:
Egyptian Magic and Christian Magic

The Copts, the Christians of Egypt, have not forgotten the ancient magic. They have reused many aspects of the rituals and magical practices which were used in pharaonic times. Christ, the Virgin Mary, the saints and angels, succeed the gods and goddesses. A large part of the ideology and symbolism called 'pagan' passed into Christianity by magic. What we call superstitions are actually ancient customs in disguise. Here one finds, pell-mell, spells for healing, for blessing the childbed, to give protection against demons, etc. The Coptic magician is an important man, a man who is heeded. Are not the patriarch and priest in some way magicians?

The Coptic magical papyri are, for the most part, Christian adaptations of earlier Egyptian works. A great spell of protection was used 'against all we know and all that we know not, against all that comes from men who are curious, cunning and cowardly'—an eternal piece of wisdom which transcends religious sects in their particularism, and awakens us today, as in the past, to the realities of the invisible. In Egyptian magic the thaumaturge takes the role of Isis. The identical process in Coptic magic occurs when the magus takes on the identity of Mary and Jesus, 'He who commands and she who speaks'.[1]

Numerous divinities have survived in Christianity. The most popular of these is Bes. In particular he appeared to the monks of the convent of Apa Moses near Abydos, in the form of a bearded demon who amused himself by pulling horrible faces.

He survives still in contemporary Egyptian folklore, in which he has become a ghost who frightens everyone, for he carries off the souls of the living into the Underworld. Bes also showed himself in a temple to the north of the convent of Apa Moses. He emerged from it and beat passers-by, leaving them one-eyed or paralysed. What's more, he took many forms. Apa brought seven brothers with him, one of whom told the story. They were in the temple one evening, praying. The earth trembled beneath them. A great uproar broke out, thunder and lightning. The Apa remained impassive—these were only a demon's sorceries, nothing more. At midnight the demon cried, 'You will not leave us to rest yet, Moses? Know that I do not fear you! Your prayers will do me no harm. You waste the night watching in vain. Flee, if you do not wish to die and make those who are with you lose their lives!' The clamour of a wailing crowd is heard, but the monks remain unmoved. The temple shakes. They fall flat on their faces but the Apa reassures them: 'Do not fear, be valiant and you will see God's glory.' The end of the tale is lost, but the outcome was obviously favourable to the holy man.

One Coptic text relates the story of the capture of some monks who were placed on the altar of a pagan temple to be sacrificed. But the Apa Bes struck the door of the temple where this crime was to be perpetrated and pronounced a magic spell: 'Great and All Powerful God, who drew Peter from prison, untied his hands and feet and made the door open before him, let not these guards hold him and let the soldiers who watch the door sleep; let the angel of the Lord follow him and lead him through the iron door leading to the town; make the temple open by itself.' The door of the sanctuary opened. The monks were released from their bonds. Apa Bes entered with fourteen monks. In unison they prayed that fire might fall from heaven. Indeed, a wall of flames surrounded the temple, then the good monks cheerfully burnt the high priest of the pagan god alive. The infidels were converted or fled into the desert.

Some texts of Christian propaganda used magic a lot, it seems, to combat the ancient Egyptian religion. Near the town of Akhmim there was a famous island where the pagans who cultivated the vines produced a bad wine which was sold at an excessive price to the workers. They complained to Apa Shenut. That night the holy man went to the island and, with a little palm branch which he held in his hand, struck a palm tree to the ground; he commanded the island to withdraw to the middle of the river and sink, like Atlantis. This was done: houses, gardens and human beings all disappeared beneath the water.[2] The legend conceals an important religious event, the suppression of the 'primordial mound' of the ancient Egyptians, symbolised by that island which also represented the pharaonic religion and its thousand-faceted magic.

Epilogue

'Magic is to know power, to know how to slip into the many forms which it takes in the world of men.' The sun was already high in the sky of Luxor when my host, the patriarch of the oldest family of magicians in Egypt, spoke these words which are so faithful to the pharaonic tradition. His wife had retired long since and his sons had gone about their work, hunting serpents and scorpions. The Old Man had done his guest the honour of remaining in his company.

Despite the lack of sleep, we were not tired. Perhaps magic, without our being aware of it, had given us its own energy, that energy which the ancient Egyptians had learnt to master in the secret places of the temples and in the Houses of Life, that power which is the true origin of the art of building.

One of the patriarch's statements will for ever be engraved on my memory: 'Magic builds man.' Not the individual, the little speck of being lost on the wave of what is possible, but Man in the image of the Cosmos, that being formed by the creative qualities of those who seek to perceive the meaning of their lives, who immerse themselves in it like the perfect swimmer of Chinese wisdom, able to float with the current without offering resistance.

Can there be anything more tempting than to sit looking at the desert beside an old magician moulded by thousands of years of experience, to watch the play of light on the sand, to abolish the frontier between the visible and the invisible? Is there a more beautiful dream than that of melting into the elusive movement of the wind which carries life as far as the dried-out hills that mark the solitude of the desert?

Yes, all of this would be easy, wonderful, enchanting . . . but the ancient Egyptians did not see the world in terms of ease. If they used magic it was because civilisation, that subtle link between all forms of life, appeared to them as a battle with reality, a daily struggle, which offered no chance of success to cowards or incompetents. A severe rule perhaps, but an implacable reality—does not our own experience of discovering the order of the world force us to just such a conclusion?

When the eyes of the Egyptian magician opened on the world they recreated it. The desert is the land of Seth the Red, the place in which is unleashed the perilous duel between uncontrolled forces who, once conquered, allow the cultivated lands to be born, the dwelling of Horus. The pharaoh, magician of magicians, is the 'third element', the One who unites the two brothers forever enemies and forever inseparable. Is not magic part of the 'King's art' which invites us, too, to mediate between heaven and earth?

List of Abbreviations

AEMT	**Borghouts, J. F.** *Ancient Egyptian Magical Texts,* **Leyden**
ASAE	*Annales du Service des Antiquités de l'Egypte,* **Cairo**
BD	*Book of the Dead*
BIFAO	*Bulletin de l'Institut Français d'Archéologie Orientale,* **Cairo**
BSFE	*Bulletin de la Société Française d'Egyptologie,* **Paris**
CdeE	*Chronique d'Egypte,* **Brussels**
CT	*Coffin Texts*
Djed-her	**Cf. Jelinkova-Raymond,** *Les inscriptions de la statue guérisseuse de Djed-her-le-Sauveur,* **Cairo 1956**
JEA	*Journal of Egyptian Archaeology,* **London**
JEOL	*'Jaarbericht van het Voorasiatisch-Egyptisch Genootschap' 'Ex Oriente Lux',* **Leiden**
JNES	*Journal of Near Eastern Studies,* **Chicago**
LdeA	*Lexikon der Ägyptologie,* **Wiesbaden**
LEXA	**Lexa, F.** *La Magie dans l'Egypte antique, de l'ancien Empire jusqu'à l'époque copte,* **3 vol., Paris 1925**
MDAIK	*Mitteilungen des Deutschen Archaeologischen Instituts, Kairo Abteilung*
OMRO	*Oudheidkundige Mededelingen uit Rikjsmuseum van Oudheiden te Leiden,* **Leiden**
Pap.Ebers	*Papyrus Ebers*

Pap.Hearst	*Hearst Medical Papyrus*
Pyr.	*Pyramid Texts*
RdeE	*Revue d'Egyptologie*
SO	*Sources Orientales*, **Editions du Seuil**
Socle	**Klasens, A.** *A Magical Statue Base (Socle Behague) in the Museum of Antiquities at Leiden,* **OMRO 33, 1952**
ZAS	*Zeitschrift für Ägyptische Sprache*

Bibliography

ALLIOT M., *Une stèle magique d'Edfou*, Mélanges Maspero I, 1934, 201–210.

ALTENMULLER H., *Matische Literatur*, LdA III, 1151–1162.

ANNEQUIN, J., *Recherches sur l'action magique et ses représentations*, Paris, 1973.

BONNET, H., *Magie, Zauber*, in RARG.

BORGHOUTS J. F., *Magie*, LdA III, 1137–1162.

—— Textes et Langages de l'Egypte pharaonique, III, Cairo, 1972, 7–19

—— *The Magical Text of Papyrus Leiden I 348*, OMRO 51, Leyden, 1971.

BOYLAN, *Thoth, the Hermes of Egypt*, Oxford, 1922.

DARESSY G., *Textes et dessins magiques*, CGC,

DAWSON, *Notes on Egyptian Magic*, Aegyptus, 1931, 23–8.

DELATTE and DERCHAIN P., *Les intailles magiques gréco-égyptiennes*, Paris, 1964.

DERCHAIN, P., *Le papyrus Salt 825 (B.M. 10051), rituel pour la conservation de la vie en Egypte*, Brussels, 1965.

ERMAN, A., *La religion des Egyptiens*, Paris, 1952.

FAULKNER R. O., *The Papyrus Bremner-Rhind*, Bibliotheca Aegyptiaca 3, Brussels, 1933 and JEA 23 (1937), 166–185 and JEA 24 (1938), 41–53.

GARDINER A. H., *Magic*, in Hastings Encyclopaedia of Religions and Ethics VIII, London, 1915, 262–9.

GOYON J.-C., *Rituels funéraires de l'ancienne Egypte*, Littératures anciennes du Proche-Orient, Paris, 1972.

GRIFFITH F. and THOMPSON H., *The Demotic Magical Papyrus of London and Leyden*, 3 vol., Oxford, 1904–1921.

—— *The Leyden Papyrus. An Egyptian Magical Book*, New York, 1974.

JELINKOVA-REYMOND E., *Les inscriptions de la statue guérisseuse de Djed-her-le-Sauveur*, Cairo, 1956.

KAKOSY L., *Heka*, LdA II, 1108–1110.

—— *Magische Stelen*, LdA III, 1162–1164.

KLASENS A., *A Magical Statue Base (Socle Behague) in the Museum of Antiquities at Leiden*, OMRO 33, 1952.

LACAU P., *Les statues guérisseuses dans l'ancienne Egypte*, Monuments Piot, XXV, 1921–22, 189–209.

LANGE H., *Der magische Papyrus Harris*, Copenhagen, 1927.

LEXA F., *La magie dans l'Egypte antique, de l'ancien Empire jusqu'à l'époque copte*, 3 vol., Paris, 1925.

MEEKS D., *Génies, anges, démons*, Sources Orientales 8, 17–84, Paris, 1971.

MASSART, *Magie*, in Dictionnaire de la Bible, Suppléments 5, 722–732, Paris, 1957.

POSENER G., *Les empreintes magiques de Gizeh et les morts dangereux*, MDAIK 16, 1958, 252–270.

—— *Princes et pays d'Asie et de Nubie*, Brussels, 1940.

—— *Les textes d'envoûtement de Mirgissa*, Syria 43, 1966, 277–287.

ROEDER G., *Zauberei und Jenseitsglauben im alten Ägypten*, Zurich, 1961.

SANDER-HANSEN C. E., *Die Texte der Metternischstele*, Copenhagen, 1956.

SAUNERON S., *Aspect d'un thème magique égyptien: les menaces incluant les dieux*, in Bulletin de la Société Française d'Egyptologie, no 8, 1951, 11–21.

—— *Le monde du magicien égyptien*, in Le monde du sorcier, Sources Orientales 7, 1966, 27–65.

—— *Les prêtres de l'ancienne Egypte*, Paris, 1957.

SEELE C., *Horus on the Crocodiles*, JNES V, 1947, 43–52.

SETHE K., *Die Achtung feindlicher Fürsten, Völker und Dinge auf altägyptischen Tongefässcherben des Mittleren Reiches*, Berlin 1926.

TE VELDE H., *The God Heka in Egyptian Theology*, JEOL 21, 1969–1970, 175 sq.

VIAUD G., *Magie et coutumes populaires chez les Coptes d'Egypte*, Sisteron, 1978.

WIEDEMANN A., *Magie and Zauberei im alten Aegypten*, Leipzig, 1905.

Notes

Chapter 1

1. Inscription no 61 from the tomb of Petosiris.
2. Hearst Medical Papyrus 11, 4,
3. Leyden Papyrus 347, 4–11.
4. C.T. I, 137 d sq.
5. C.T. Spell 1 017.
6. *Dictionnaire de la civilisation égyptienne*, 278.
7. Pyr. Spell 273–274.
8. Pyr. § 1 324,
9. Pyr. § 477.
10. Pyr. § 924.
11. Leyden Magical Papyrus, 42.
12. ASAE 39, 57 sq.
13. Papyrus Salt 825, 5–6.
14. *Id.*, 139.
15. Lexa I, 145.
16. Pyr. § 1 100.
17. C.T. Spell 1 087.
18. C.T. Spell 281.
19. Goyon, *Rituels*, 257–8.
20. BD chap. 135.
21. C.T. Spell 503.
22. Lexa II, 50.
23. ZAS 57, 70.
24. C.T. Spells 370 and 374.

Chapter 2

1. JEOL 23, 359.
2. *De Abstinentia* IV, 6.
3. Goyon, *Rituels*, 258–9.
4. Sauneron, *Pap. mag. ill. Brooklyn*, 20, note 1^2 (b).
5. Apology, XXVI.
6. Goyon, *Rituels*, 178.
7. BD Spell 42.
8. OMRO 51, 19–20.
9. Djed-her, 34.
10. Lexa II, 59.
11. Lexa II, 74 (Metternich stela).
12. C.T. II, 37.
13. I, 71 and 49.
14. Leyden Magical Papyrus, 45.
15. Goyon, *Rituels*, 74.
16. ASAE 39, 70–71.
17. Derchain, *Pap. Salt* 825, 35.
18. BIFAO 40, 98–99.
19. BD Spell 64.
20. BD Spell 125.
21. BD Spell 80.
22. Derchain, *Pap. Salt* 825, 171.
23. BD Spell 163.
24. C.T. Spell 1 018.
25. e.g. 1 054, 1 055, 1 057.
26. C.T. Spell 396–397.
27. BD Spell 68.
28. C.T. Spell 91.
29. Goyon, *Rituels*, 179.
30. C.T. Spell 30.
31. Title to Spell 467 of the C.T.

Chapter 3

1. Beginning of Spell 349 of C.T.
2. Turin Papyrus 118, 9–10.
3. Sauneron, *Prêtres*, 62.
4. Leyden Papyrus 348, Recto 2, 1.
5. E. Drioton, *la Protection magique de Thèbes à l' époque des Ptolémées, in l' Ethnographie*, 1931, 3–10.
6. AEMT, 11.
7. C.T. VI, 71.
8. Pyr. § 134= C.T. I, 187.
9. Cf. J.-C. Goyon, *le Papyrus du Louvre N 3 279*, 75.
10. Sauneron, *Pap. mag. illustré Brooklyn*, 1920, note I',
11. ASAE 39, 75.
12. Derchain, *Pap. Salt*, 144.
13. *Id.*, 90.
14. SO 8, 27.
15. Goyon, *Rituels*, 61.
16. Goyon, *le Papyrus du Louvre N 3 279*, 34.
17. Goyon, *Rituels*, 205.
18. Posener, RdE 22, 204.
19. Lexa II, 51–52.
20. Posener, RdE 5, 51–56.
21. C.T. Spell 410 and 412.
22. C.T. 238.
23. C.T. Spell 220, for example.
24. C.T. Spell 24.
25. BD Spell 125.
26. BD Spell 153 A.

Chapter 4

1. OMRO 51, 10.
2. Erman et Ranke, *Civilisation*, 458.
3. BD, spell 137 A.
4. Djed-her, 9–14.

5. H. Altenmuller, *Die Apotropaia und die Götter Mittelä-gyptens*, 1965.
6. Lexa I, 88.
7. SO 8, 55–6.
8. BD, spell 101.
9. Goyon, *Rituels*, 73.
10. *Id,*, 51.
11. Daumas, BIFAO LIX, 72–3.
12. Goyon, *Rituels*, 49.
13. Lexa II, 136.
14. Drioton, *Miscellanea Gregoriana*, 73 sq.
15. Leyden Magical Papyrus, 33–5.
16. LdA III, 1 138.
17. Cf. Schneider, *Shabtis*.
18. C.T. spell 472.
19. Cf. Gardiner/Sethe, *Egyptian Letters to the Dead*, 1928.
20. Guilmot, ZAS 99, 94 sq.
21. Leyden Magical Papyrus 47–51.

Chapter 5

1. Pyr., spell 353.
2. Goyon, *Rituels*, 260.
3. C.T. IV 115, 124, 136.
4. C.T. I, 188.
5. Beginning of spell 76 of C.T.
6. Leyden Magical Papyrus.
7. BD spell 130.
8. C.T. spell 361.
9. AEMT, 89.
10. Goyon, *Rituels*, 70.
11. Goyon, *Le pap. Louvre N 3 279*, 53–54.
12. C.T. spell 840.
13. Pyr., spell 406.
14. Lexa II, 70 (Metternich stela).
15. Djed-her, 50–2.
16. CdE XLV, 253; AEMT, 87.

17. AEMT, 86.
18. Pap. Harris IV, 6–7.
19. AEMT, 89.
20. C.T. spell 297.
21. C.T. spell 162.
22. C.T. spell 80.
23. AEMT, 14–15.
24. Socle 61.
25. OMRO 51, 13,
26. AEMT, 25.
27. Erman, *Religion*, 343.
28. Lexa II, 31,
29. Book of repulsing Apophis, 23, 14 sq.
30. Lexa II, 97.
31. Derchain, *Pap. Salt*, 141.
32. Djed-her, 41.
33. C.T. spell 311.
34. C.T. spell 1 032–1 033.
35. C.T. spell 100.
36. C.T. spell 758–9.
37. C.T. spell 246.
38. C.T. spell 284.
39. C.T. spell 288.
40. C.T. spell 1 130.
41. BD spell 162.
42. BD spell 137 A.

Chapter 6

1. Goyon, *Rituels*, 259.
2. Lexa II, 66.
3. Djed-her, 49–50.
4. Socle, 62–3.
5. Lexa II, 81 (Metternich stela).
6. Pyr. 962–3.
7. Lexa II, 41.
8. Faulkner, *An Ancient Book of Hours*, 20, 25 a 21, 5.

9. Pyr. 954–5.
10. Pyr., spell 678.
11. C.T. spell 992.
12. C.T. I, 231.
13. C.T. I, 210–11.
14. Goyon, *Rituels*, 248.
15. Sauneron, *Pap. mag. ill. Brooklyn*. 15–16.
16. ASAE 39, 75.
17. AEMT, 75.
18. AEMT, 82–3.
19. Lexa II, 76.
20. AEMT, 70.
21. Erman, *Religion*, 343.
22. C.T. spell 269.
23. SO 8, 56–7.
24. C.T. I, 314–321.
25. C.T. spell 81.
26. OMRO 51, 16–17.
27. BD spell 54.
28. Goyon, *Rituels*, 76.
29. AEMT, 37.
30. Lexa I, 166.
31. SO 8, 53–4.
32. Brooklyn mag. pap. 47 218, 156, second document.
33. Socle, 58–9.
34. Lexa II, 74.
35. Sander-Hansen, *Die religiosen Texten auf dem Sarg des Anchenesneferibre*, 1937, 118 (372).
36. BD spell 164.
37. SO 8, 44.
38. AEMT, 15.
39. Yoyotte, BSFE 87–8, 47 sq.
40. AEMT, 39.
41. AEMT, 90.
42. Sauneron, *Pap. mag. ill. Brooklyn*, 11–12.
43. *Id.*, 13.
44. *Id.*, 26, note 4[4] (n).

Chapter 7

1. For a complete collection of these tales and legends cf. Lefebvre, *Romans et contes de l'Egypte pharaonique* and Lichtheim, *Ancient Egyptian Literature*, I–III.
2. Lexa II, 198–206.
3. *Id.*, 71.
4. Djed-her, 54–55.
5. Socle, 79.
6. Sauneron, *Pap. mag. ill. Brooklyn*, 24.
7. AEMT, 7–10.
8. Lexa II, 95.
9. BD spell 7.
10. ASAE 39, 80.
11. AEMT, 18.
12. In the tradition of the C.T.
13. Altenmüller, *Die Apotropaia*.
14. AEMT, 2.
15. C.T. spell 392.
16. SO 7, 47.
17. *Id.*
18. Erman, *Religion*, 351.
19. Syria XLIII, 277 sq.
20. C.T. spell 37.
21. Pap. Jumilhac XVIII, 9–11.
22. AEMT, 2.
23. AEMT, 1.
24. Leyden mag. pap. 145–7.
25. *Id.*, 109.
26. SO 7, 60, n. 39.
27. Socle, 60.
28. AEMT, 6.
29. Pap. Turin, 137, 2–4.
30. Pap. Chester Beatty V, verso 5, 4–6, 4.
31. OMRO 51, 28.
32. Lexa II, 57.
33. AEMT, 80.

34. J.-C. Goyon, *Pap. Louvre N 3 279*, 42–3.
35. AEMT, 3.
36. AEMT, 4.
37. OMRO 51, 33.

Chapter 8

1. Djed-her, 36.
2. Socle, 57.
3. OMRO 51, 12.
4. Pap. Ebers 2, 1–2, 6.
5. Erman, *Religion*, 340.
6. AEMT, 45.
7. Pap. Ebers [3] 2, 1–6.
8. *Id.*, [2] 1. 12–2, 1.
9. Erman-Ranke, *Civilisation*, 459.
10. AEMT, 81.
11. AEMT, 37.
12. Pap. Ebers 90, 15–91, 1 = RdE 9, 60.
13. Leyden mag. pap. 127.
14. Erman-Ranke, *Civilisation*, 470.
15. Pyr., spell 533.
16. AEMT, 29.
17. Goyon, *Rituels*, 45.
18. ASAE 39, 68–9.
19. AEMT, 23.
20. AEMT, 24.
21. Leyden mag. pap. 177.
22. OMRO 51, 23.
23. Lexa II, 149.
24. AEMT, 30.
25. OMRO 51, 18.
26. AEMT, 31.
27. SO 7, 43.
28. SO 7, 37.
29. Goyon, *Rituels*, 245.
30. AEMT, 32.

31. AEMT, 22.
32. AEMT, 33.
33. Goyon, *Rituels*, 148 and 150 note 2.
34. Pap. Ebers [360] 58, 6–15.
35. London Papyrus 7, 1–7, 8.
36. AEMT, 47–48.
37. Pap. Ebers, 58, 6-58, 15.
38. BD spell 140.
39. AEMT, 88.
40. Borghouts, *The Evil Eye of Apophis*, JEA 59, 1973, 114–150.
41. Lexa III, pl. XII.
42. Pyr., spell 211.
43. Goyon, *Rituels*, 167–8.
44. Pap. Hearst [215] 14, 7–10.
45. AEMT, 32.
46. OMRO 51, 27.
47. C.T. spell 341.
48. OMRO 51, 26.
49. Socle, 54.
50. Goyon, *Rituels*, 62, 48.
51. Derchain, Pap. Salt 825, no 325.
52. Pap. Ebers [811] 95, 7–14.
53. ASAE 39, 70.
54. Leyden mag. pap. 149.
55. AEMT, 83.
56. C.T. IV, 183.

Chapter 9

1. AEMT, 1.
2. Lexa II, 155–6.
3. Lexa I, 165.
4. Leyden mag. pap. 89.
5. *Id.*. 137.
6. OMRO 51, 30.
7. AEMT, 39–40.

8. OMRO 51, 13.
9. Lexa II, 29.
10. OMRO 51, 31.
11. SO 8, 51–2.
12. Lexa II, 32–33.
13. AEMT, 42.
14. *Id.*
15. *Id.*, 43.
16. Lexa II, 29.
17. AEMT, 70.
18. Socle, 58.
19. *Id.*, 82.
20. OMRO, 51, 25.
21. Erman, *Religion*, 349.
22. Desroches-Noblecourt, RdE 9, 49–67.
23. Erman-Ranke, *Civilisation*, 455.
24. Goyon, *Rituels*, 308.

Chapter 10

1. C.T. 148–50.
2. *Id.*, IV, 73.
3. *Id.*, IV, 148.
4. Djed-her, 81–4.
5. AEMT, 38.
6. Leyden mag. pap. 123.
7. T. Save-Soderbergh, *On Egyptian Representations of Hippo-potamus hunting as a Religious Motive*, Horae Soederblomi-anae, Uppsala, 1953.
8. Pap. Ebers, 88, 13–6.
9. Leyden mag. pap. 39.
10. C.T. spell 342; BD spell 31–2.
11. AEMT, 83.
12. *Id.*, 86–7.
13. SO 7, 44.
14. Leyden mag. pap. 37.
15. AEMT, 78.

16. Djed-her, 133.
17. *Id.*, 15—18.
18. AEMT, 77.
19. BIFAO 78, 451.
20. Lexa II, 72—3.
21. Cf., e.g. A. ROCATTI, Papiro ieratico n. 54 003, Turin, 1970.
22. ASAE 39, 77 and 80.
23. Djed-her, 26—7.
24. Goyon, *Pap. du Louvre N 3 279*, 31 and n. 3.
25. Djed-her, 39.
26. AEMT, 94.
27. Djed-her, 53.
28. AEMT, 91.
29. Socle, 80—1.
30. SO 8, 43.
31. Djed-her, 33.
32. BD spell 87.
33. Djed-her, 34—5.
34. *Id.*, 45.
35. AEMT, 78 and 81.
36. Djed-her, 43.
37. AEMT, 59.
38. *Id.*, 82.
39. Pap. mag. Harris, 8, 5.
40. Leyden mag. pap. 131—3.
41. *Id.*, 125.
42. *Id.*, 129—131.
43. *Id.*, 37.
44. AEMT, 16.

Appendix

1. Socle, 67.
2. For all the foregoing, cf. Lexa II 217—230.